How to be a Reflexive Researcher

Paul Hibbert

University of St Andrews, UK

Edward Elgar
PUBLISHING

Cheltenham, UK • Northampton, MA, USA

Published by
Edward Elgar Publishing Limited
The Lypiatts
15 Lansdown Road
Cheltenham
Glos GL50 2JA
UK

Edward Elgar Publishing, Inc.
William Pratt House
9 Dewey Court
Northampton
Massachusetts 01060
USA

Paperback edition 2022

A catalogue record for this book
is available from the British Library

Library of Congress Control Number: 2021946163

This book is available electronically in the **Elgar**online
Business subject collection
http://dx.doi.org/10.4337/9781839101854

ISBN 978 1 83910 184 7 (cased)
ISBN 978 1 83910 185 4 (eBook)
ISBN 978 1 0353 0905 4 (paperback)

Printed and bound by CPI Group (UK) Ltd, Croydon, CR0 4YY

Contents

Tables

Acknowledgements

I have long believed that everything we achieve is collaborative in some sense, since we depend on and are shaped by our networks of relationships. This book is no exception and for that reason I would like to offer my thanks to all those who have helped me along the way. First and foremost, I would like to thank the University of St Andrews for allowing me the time to complete this project, along with the University of Auckland for providing a welcoming home from home (and a shelter from the Scottish winter).

I would also like to thank the helpful and kind publishing team at Edward Elgar – including Emily Mew, Francine O'Sullivan, Ellen Pearce and Finn Halligan – for their patience in the face of delays to this project caused by global and personal circumstances. There will be numerous others behind the scenes to whom I have not been introduced, but I send you all my sincere thanks too.

In turning to academic colleagues and friends I cannot mention everyone who I have been lucky enough to connect with (and no slight is intended) since parts of this book are shaped by my whole academic career. Of those I am able to mention, I would like to give the first mention to Chris Huxham, an inspiring and challenging doctoral supervisor and colleague. Other colleagues that helped me to make a start as an academic include Christine Coupland, Thomas Diefenbach, Colin Eden, Robert MacIntosh, Peter McInnes, Aidan McQuade, John and Joe Raelin, John Sillince, Jörg Sydow and especially Ann Cunliffe, who paved the way for so many of us to engage with reflexivity. In recent years I have been lucky enough to work with more great scholars such as Lisa Anderson, Bill Foster, Danna Greenberg, Ben Hardy, Hee-Sun Kim, Stefan Korber, Dirk Lindebaum, Katy Mason, Christine Rivers, Ziad El Sahn and Lotta Windahl. I must thank Nic Beech, Lisa Callagher, Frank Siedlok and April Wright most of all, because it has been so transformative to work with them. This book would have been impossible without their collaboration in recent research projects and their supportive friendship.

Some reflexive research projects seem to have their roots in our family lives and that has obviously been true in the case of this book. With that in mind, I conclude by sending my warmest thoughts to my sisters and brothers – Sue, Chris, Peter and Mark – who made it through the same challenging times.

1. Introduction: how to be a reflexive researcher

My father was shouting at my mother, after coming home drunk, as I stepped into the room. I was seven years old and frightened. I started to cry. That was the first time my father called me a "fucking little queer".
As time passed fear turned to hate; I learned to loathe everything about him. I noticed his rolling macho gait... and made sure I walked in a very upright way. Hearing his noisy breathing when he was drunk and asleep in an armchair, I monitored my breathing to make sure it was inaudible. He was a prodigious drinker and was foul-mouthed – before I left the family home when I was eighteen, I refused to either drink or swear. This confused my few friends in the last couple of years at high school, most of whom would somehow smuggle the occasional beer here or there... and away from class their language was pretty unrestrained. It took me a long time to loosen up.

1.1 REFLEXIVITY IS A PERSONAL PROJECT

There are lots of ways of looking at reflexivity, but for me it is at heart a personal project. We all change in response to experience (even if it is not always as extreme a reaction as described in the autobiographical excerpt above) and that is the essence of reflexivity. It is a process of engaging with experience, that changes our ways of understanding and guides adaptation in readiness for future experiences. This has implications for our everyday life, but also for the understandings on which interpretive research processes are built. With that in mind I used the brief autobiographical except above above as an illustration because it shows how changing in response to experience can include four levels, even in relation to one small event:

- *Embodied* (my seven-year-old self amongst adults)
- *Emotional* (fear and crying)
- *Rational* (decisions about undesirable behaviours like drinking)
- *Relational* (interactions with my father, mother and friends).

These are important insights for reflexive practice in research, which I will develop in detail later in this book.

Looking back there are other things, that I could not have known, that follow from my response to the experience narrated above. I would certainly not have characterised them as an example of reflexivity, for a start – that is not in the vocabulary of the average schoolkid. I was also unaware of all the effects that would flow from my choices, as well as being far less aware of less dramatic influences on how I changed as I grew up – the encouragement from particular teachers, my mother working hard to keep us all going, enthusiasms developed from reading. However, my main point here is not to dwell any further on my personal life, but instead – hopefully – to provide some resonance with your own experiences and responses, in order to emphasise the ordinariness and universality of reflexivity. This means that when we seek to become a reflexive researcher, there is a lot that we may be able to build on, but also quite a lot to unpack.

In academic conversations about reflexivity in research, we are often concerned to do one of two things. One alternative is to try to compensate for the 'skew' in our perspective, that causes us to see things in a certain individual way that may be atypical; for example, think of my teenage schoolfriends' bewilderment of my refusal to indulge in the occasional smuggled beer. Another alternative is to try to speak authentically from our experience; for example, I might be able to speak and write about angry and abusive fathers, in a way that others might find meaningful. Either of these alternatives is a possible way of being a reflexive researcher, especially if you are working within or from the interpretive tradition. With that in mind, the main purposes of this book are to set out the academic debates behind each position, develop a picture of reflexive practice that enables either approach to be adopted, and consider the issues and implications that follow from each approach. In the remainder of this introductory chapter, I outline how the book is arranged in order to fulfil those objectives. It is likely that the outline will raise questions that the detailed chapters that follow will answer.

1.2   ENGAGING WITH THE FIELD: THE ACADEMIC PROJECT

In the text above I have emphasised how reflexivity is a personal project. However, much of the literature in the field is concerned with the 'academic project' and how reflexivity is used in the service of our research. This is an important topic for all qualitative researchers and interpretive researchers in particular, who are called to account for the personal and intellectual means by which they develop their insights (Schwartz-Shea & Yanow, 2012).

Chapter 2 explains how reflexivity is approached in the literature in a number of ways, largely focussed around four themes. *Self-reflexivity* focusses on the everyday processes of individual adaptation that are guided by our interpretation of experience (Archer, 2007; Caetano, 2017; Hibbert, Coupland & MacIntosh, 2010; Hibbert, Beech & Siedlok, 2017). *Critical reflexivity* seeks to identify the social constructions of tradition and ideology that shape our interpretations of experience, to interrupt and challenge the unquestioned norms that we carry and reproduce in this way (Aronowitz, Deener, Keene, Schnittker & Tach, 2015; Hibbert, Beech & Siedlok, 2017; Hibbert, Coupland & MacIntosh, 2010; Hibbert & Huxham, 2010, 2011). *Relational reflexivity* considers the interdependence of individuals in social contexts, the ways in which our thinking is shaped by the influence and insights of others, and how we influence them in turn (Hibbert, Sillince, Diefenbach & Cunliffe, 2014; Cutcher, Hardy, Riach & Thomas, 2020). *Radical reflexivity* takes the principles of self and critical reflexivity to their ultimate conclusion by denying robust foundational truths or easily generalisable insights about how we live in and interpret the world, in favour of local, subjective explanations (Cunliffe, 2003). An additional (and somewhat implicit) theme is *instrumental reflexivity*, which provides a balance or contrast to radical reflexivity by using the principles of critical reflexivity in a constrained and focussed approach, to remove less robust or persuasive insights about how we live in and interpret the world (Alvesson, Hardy & Harley, 2008; Weick, 1999).

Chapter 2 goes on to show how the ways in which reflexivity can be described and enacted, as described above and applied most often in interpretive research, can also be gathered into two broader categories. The first category emerges through considering the example of ethnographic and autoethnographic research approaches. Such approaches depend (in part) on capturing how reflexivity is used to shape our future, as we adapt to our way of being with our research participants in their environments and change our research practice accordingly (Beech, Hibbert, McInnes & MacIntosh, 2009). These approaches bring together insights focussed on self-reflexivity and relational reflexivity (Archer, 2007; Cutcher, Hardy, Riach & Thomas, 2020; Hibbert, Coupland & MacIntosh, 2010; Hibbert, Sillince, Diefenbach & Cunliffe, 2014). These two forms integrate as *future-oriented reflexivity*, focussed on how we actively change and develop, in response to the ways that we interpret our experience of the world from moment to moment. In future-oriented reflexivity, changes in the researcher's ways of being and doing are the most important outcomes and sources of insight (Hibbert, Beech, Callagher & Siedlok, 2021).

The second category, focussing on how interpretive researchers seek to use reflexivity to look back on research experiences, to challenge their interpretations, brings together insights focussed on instrumental reflexivity, critical reflexivity and radical reflexivity (Alvesson, Hardy & Harley, 2008; Cunliffe, 2003; Weick, 1999). Taking these themes together brings a different process into view. Although these approaches have different philosophical commitments and limits, they are all concerned with looking below the surface assumptions of past experience, to see how social and historical contexts have shaped us and our interpretations without any deliberate action on our part (Cunliffe, 2004; Hibbert, Coupland & MacIntosh, 2010). This kind of engagement with our interpretive and formative hinterland (Hibbert, Beech & Siedlok, 2017) can be characterised as *past-oriented reflexivity*.

While Chapter 2 addresses the major themes in the literature and develops new categorisations, it does not dwell in detail on the philosophical and paradigmatic debates that are common in the field, for reasons that are set out later. There are other treatments available if your interest tends in that direction, but a detailed engagement with those debates is not necessary for the main purposes of this book to be fulfilled. Instead, the focus in Chapter 2 is to outline themes and categories that can provide an initial handle on what reflexivity may mean, and how we can understand the ways in which it can connect to research projects. In that way, Chapter 2 provides the groundwork for considering in more detail how reflexivity, as an intellectual objective, can be translated into reflexive practice.

1.3   OUTLINING REFLEXIVE PRACTICES

The characterisation of reflexive practices that flow from theoretical under-standings is set out in Chapter 3. The discussion in that chapter connects to the categorisations of reflexivity developed in Chapter 2, but of necessity includes additional, interdisciplinary engagements in relation to some of the major themes. Some of these engagements step beyond the bounds of established debate and in the field.

Chapter 3 builds up a characterisation and discussion of four levels of (overlapping) reflexive practice, namely *embodied, emotional, rational* and *relational*. While it is possible to argue for a more holistic conceptualisation, or to integrate a point of view using one kind of reflexive practice as the key (for example, rational reflexive practice could be focussed on developing an account of experiences at the other levels – and often is), my argument is that it makes a practical difference to consider the levels individually in the first instance.

Embodied reflexive practice involves developing a focus on *interoception* (Hardy & Hibbert, 2012; Tsakiris & De Preester, 2019), the awareness we have of what is going on within our bodies, which has often been seen to be less relevant than external information (Leder, 2019). This is a complex and emergent area of biological and medical science and provides a different perspective from those that interpretivist scholars are generally familiar with. I encourage you not to reach for the 'incommensurability' shield, but instead to engage with the interesting insights that are being developed in this field. The research in this area is in fact highly relevant, leading to important insights in a number of areas, such as: a link between emotions and our interoceptive experiences (Berntson, Gianaros & Tsakiris, 2019); the relationship between better interoceptive awareness and the regulation of our emotions (Critchley & Harrison, 2013); links between aroused bodily states and interpretations of human interactions (Hardy & Hibbert, 2012); our experience of the passage of time (Wittman & Meissner, 2019); the connection between interoception and our sense of the outside world that influences the stability of our sense of self. All of these insights are obviously important for the study of reflexivity, bringing to light both how we adapt in response to external experiences in and through the responses of our bodies, as well as how our bodies can shape how we gather experiences in the first place. As discussed in Chapter 3, the theme of embodied reflexive practice also has a strong connection to the level of emotional reflexive practice and, in some ways, sets the stage for that.

Research has also begun to direct substantial attention towards emotion and reflexivity as an important theme in its own right, with some suggesting that emotions are the basis for reflexive thought and practice (Archer, 2007; Burkitt, 2012; Holmes, 2010). In addition, some specific areas of research in the social sciences are naturally and focally concerned with emotion, such as studies that look at dying and suffering (Evans, Ribbens McCarthy, Bowlby, Wouangoa & Kébé, 2017; Miller, 2002), while most areas of human behaviour worthy of study in social and organisational contexts necessarily involve emotion on some level (Lindebaum, 2017). Emotions are, however, complex and entangled with physiological and cognitive processes (Immordino-Yang, 2016) and thus reflexive practice focussing on emotional *perceptions* can impact dramatically on how situations and possibilities for action are interpreted and understood (Brown & de Graaf, 2013). Building on this, there are a range of specific ways in which emotions can be connected to reflexive practice, especially when the situation calls for some significant change in understanding and approach to action (Hibbert, Callagher, Siedlok, Windahl & Kim, 2019) and there is also a strong link to debates about what is entailed in self-reflexivity in the context of remembered experiences (Corlett, 2013). Overall, the role of both negative and positive perceptions of emotion (Brown & de Graaf, 2013; Hibbert, Beech, Callagher & Siedlok, 2021; Shin, 2014) that can proceed rational thought are an essential focus for reflexive practice, and Chapter 3 focusses on emotional reflexive practice and attention to emotional perceptions in some detail.

The most familiar conceptualisations of reflexive practice are, however, concerned with rational thought. Indeed, rational reflexivity often encompasses what people mean by reflexivity as such, and can be imagined as a process of 'thinking about our thinking', to examine how and why we interpret things in the ways that we do (Hibbert, Coupland & MacIntosh, 2010). Framed in that way, rational reflexive practice is a matter of choice in everyday life and especially in the situations of research, in which it can be mobilised selectively and deliberately and operationalised through specific frameworks or tools (Alvesson, Hardy & Harley, 2008; Weick, 1999). However, approaches to rational reflexive practice may also have strong relational and/ or emotional overlaps too (Ripamonti, Galuppo, Gorli, Scaratti & Cunliffe, 2017). However, all of the varieties of rational reflexive practice tend to be concerned with the same underlying focus, namely opening up our patterns of interpretation to critical examination in order to see the social, ideological and traditional influences in our formative past that have shaped them (Hibbert, Beech & Siedlok, 2017; Hibbert & Huxham, 2010, 2011; McLean, Harvey & Chia, 2012; Sklaveniti & Steyaert, 2020).

Rational reflexive practice always runs up against the problem of having no neutral place to stand from which to examine our own formation (Cunliffe, 2003; Hibbert, Coupland & MacIntosh, 2010), meaning that our accounts are less transparent with regard to their influences and sources than we would like them to be. However, enhanced awareness of what is going on in the process of interpretation helps us to break open *apperception*, by allowing us to show how we *contextualise* our interpretations (showing where they come from) so that we can give an account of the patterns behind our *conceptualisations* (the ways in which we choose to describe our interpretation of experience). The focus on rational reflexivity in Chapter 3 is therefore on opening up the usually automatic process of apperception, to allow some light on the tightly linked and overlapping practices of contextualisation and conceptualisation. Doing so allows us to consider how a more deliberate engagement can hold these practices apart, at least to a degree, and so make space for a more honest account of our situated experience (Iszatt-White, Kempster & Carroll, 2017).

The final aspect of reflexive practice is the relational level, which has many overlaps with embodied, emotional and rational aspects of reflexive practice (Adjepong, 2019; Ripamonti, Galuppo, Gorli, Scaratti & Cunliffe, 2017). In addition, at the relational level there can be self-reflexive, interpersonal and collective conceptualisations, involving a complex choreography of moving between and relying on the self and others (Nicholls, 2009). However, it is the engagement between the self and the other, with the intent to support the possibility of learning and the development of a shared horizon of understanding, which is key (Hibbert, Beech & Siedlok, 2017; Hibbert, Sillince, Diefenbach & Cunliffe, 2014). These possibilities can be enacted in different ways through dialogue (Hibbert, Beech & Siedlok, 2017; Simon, 2013), the use of media as a common focus (Ajjawi, Hilder, Noble, Teodorczuk & Billett, 2020), or the juxtaposition of different interpretive frames (Keevers & Treleaven, 2011).

Whether connections are established through dialogue, transitional objects or other forms of interaction, learning and change can follow (Bissett & Saunders, 2015). This involves a letting go (at least for a time) of one's own interpretive authority, in order to *receive* new insights from the other, which needs to be followed by *resolution* through dialogue until the partners in the exchange believe they have established a shared interpretive horizon (Hibbert, Sillince, Diefenbach & Cunliffe, 2014; Rhodes & Carlsen, 2018). The practices of reception and resolution that are intrinsic to relational reflexive practice are important in helping to establish enlarged understandings. These insights are richer and deeper because, through dialogue, they connect to and reveal something of the 'hinterland' of each partner's understanding (Lupu, Spence & Empson, 2018).

It is important to emphasise that, like reflexivity in general, all of the levels of reflexivity – *embodied, emotional, rational* and *relational* – can be more or less 'automatic'. We are always adapting to experience whether it affects us through our bodies, emotions, thoughts or relationships. But an awareness of what is going on at these levels lets us interrupt the automatic processes, in order to give an enriched account of our interpretations and choices, which is important for everyday reflexive practice and essential for interpretive research.

1.4 APPLYING REFLEXIVE PRACTICES TO RESEARCH PROJECTS

Chapter 4 considers how everyday reflexive practices can have a role across the full duration of a research project, stretching from the initial motivation to engage in a study to the processes of writing and revision on the way to producing published accounts of the research. The chapter describes what might be considered one kind of 'ideal type' of interpretive research process, that proceeds through clear steps in a more-or-less linear way. While lived-out experience of research projects is often more disordered and a lot less predictable, all projects tend to involve arrangements of the steps or phases that are set out in Chapter 4.

The 'ideal type' or organising framework for a research process that I set out in the chapter involves seven research phases or activities. First, I describe the initial characterisation of the research idea and the commitment that we develop before any formal project is underway. I explain how this can be either 'hot' or 'cold' – driven from emotional reflexive practice and deep personal engagement with the research question, or from an analytical focus on literature emphasising rational reflexive practice, tempered by relational reflexive practice to challenge the research ideas that we develop.

Second, I explore the grounding of a potential project in literature to give it shape and provide a clear research focus. There are a range of skills deployed in assembling and working with literature, but underpinning these is a pattern of rational reflexive practice involving apperception – interpreting new ideas in the context of what we already know, to be able to conceptualise our own view of the field – that we can engage with in a deliberate way. I also argue that relational reflexive practice has a role in shaping how a project is grounded in literature, through providing different views on our appropriation of literature, such that we can develop plausible generative speculations about where the planned research should focus.

The third element is concerned with the identification of the context(s) in which a study can be conducted. I argue that 'hot motivations' and research initiated by emotional perceptions will likely lead directly to the situations that led to the heat as the most appropriate contexts for the study. In contrast, 'cold motivations' are likely to lead to rationally reflexive practice to guide the selection of research site(s), through determining fit with our established contextualisation of the field.

In the fourth element, choices about data – how it is identified, delimited and captured – are considered. There are potential arguments about the role of embodiment and emotions in leading us to data, especially in field research. In response, I describe how relational reflexive practice helps us to establish spatial boundaries for data collection, while rational reflexive practice can help us to identify the temporal limits.

Approaches to analysis are discussed in the fifth part of the chapter, with an eye on how we develop meaningful insights from data or empirical material. I focus on appropriate forms for arranging and reporting data that includes observations developed (in whole or part) through embodied and emotional reflexive practice, and consider how relational and rational reflexive practices can help us to ensure that the accounts of our data that we craft can resonate with others as authentic views on the research context(s).

In the sixth element I explore the process of reconnecting to literature as we seek to show how meaningful insights, developed from data, can take the academic conversation in a new direction. I explain how this is a complex interplay between our own rational reflexive practice and relational reflexive practice in which we treat authors, through their texts, as partners in a generative conversation about our work. Through this conversational mode of engagement, that allows for a 'fusion of horizons' (Gadamer, 1998; Hibbert, Beech & Siedlok, 2017), the *possibility* of shared understanding in relation to our intellectual contribution is developed.

The final element of the research process that I consider is the necessity of engaging in and reacting to debate as our work is challenged and reshaped during dissemination and publication processes. As with the previous element, I see this as another complex interplay between our own rational reflexive practice and relational reflexive practice, this time with reviewers, editors and perhaps audiences during conference presentations or workshops. However, I also discuss how it is difficult to avoid some embodied and emotional engagement during this process, especially if it proves to be challenging. I do not think that is necessarily a bad thing, and we may be right in some cases to trust how we feel about our work, rather than what others say about it.

The discussions about the role of reflexive practices in research processes, as set out above, cover pretty much every aspect other than ethical review procedures – those are matters that need to be addressed on an institutional level, in most cases since most have their own specific frameworks. Despite this broad scope, it is important to emphasise that I am not seeking to provide a comprehensive guide to qualitative research, or to argue for a particular style of interpretive research or to describe in detail a particular method (as I have done with colleagues elsewhere: see, for example, Hibbert, Sillince, Diefenbach & Cunliffe, 2014). Instead, my aim is simply to show the role that reflexive practices can and should have in each of these processes. The aim is therefore to help readers consider how reflexive practices might be useful within their own research approach, especially if they are required to account for the choices that they make in particular projects.

While Chapter 4 emphasises the role of particular reflexive practices in different research activities or phases, it is important to note that all of the types of reflexive practice are potentially active at any time, but they may have more-or-less salience for the particular activities on which we are seeking to focus from moment to moment. The reflexive practices will also vary in relation to the nature of particular projects, and the seven principal activities of the 'ideal type' of research process may be combined and blended in different ways. To begin to explore some of the potential variations, Chapter 4 is followed by two case study chapters.

1.5   PERSPECTIVES: VIEWS ON REFLEXIVE PRACTICE IN RESEARCH CASE STUDIES

In Chapters 5 and 6, I look at my own lived experience of reflexive practice through two case studies. In each of these chapters, I use the framework set out in Chapter 4 to describe the study, but with variations to reflect the different shape of each study. It is important to point out at this stage that the cases were selected to provide as much variation as possible, within the scope of my career, but I have always focussed on interpretive research. With that in mind I selected my doctoral research project from many years ago, together with a collaborative research project that was approaching publication at the same time that this book was on the way to completion.

The exploration of my doctoral research in Chapter 5 presented me with some challenges. The first and most significant of these challenges was the need to 'retro-fit' my current understanding of reflexivity and reflexive practice on to a time when my engagement with those ideas was much less developed. Given the need to engage with case material intimately in order to comment on reflexive practice – with an awareness of embodied, emotional, rational and relational levels – I have some concerns about the possibility of 'getting in touch with the experience' after a great deal of time. However, as later work with colleagues has shown (Hibbert, Beech, Callagher & Siedlok, 2021) very strong emotional perceptions tend to persist, and these helped to pull me back in to the experience of that time. So, while it would not have been possible for me to write an account of my research in the same way at the time it was being conducted, I believe that I have rendered an authentic account based on memory, research notes, draft writings and various other items of research documentation.

I considered that my doctoral research might be a useful case study for some of the readers of this book, who may themselves be researching their thesis, but more importantly it provides good examples of four challenges that are more general. First, in doctoral research studies we are usually expected to focus on supporting the generalisability of our insights and this reflexive practice can be focussed on that objective, in which we try to defend rather than own our inter-pretations of data, and that challenge is often faced in publication processes for other kinds of research project too. Second, research projects are usually imprecise and imperfect, with occasional changes of direction and missed opportunities (in general, and in relation to reflexive practice) and my doctoral research provides a good example of that normal level of messiness. Third, I hope to make this book useful for a wide range of researchers within the interpretive tradition, and since my research was focussed on widely applied social theory in multiple regional, national and international network contexts, it provides a lot of possibilities for connection across a range of disciplines. Fourth, while my doctoral research was based on data collected through a fairly common approach to participant observation, it had an unusual structure and a non-standard approach to analysis. Since accounting for the structure and methodology of the study are key issues in formal doctoral examinations and studies on the way to publication, my hope is that the account of how I wrestled with these issues in my research may resonate with and be useful to others.

The conclusion I reach from the consideration of my doctoral work is that reflexive practices do not need, necessarily, to be understood and named according to my scheme (or any other) in order to go on. However, I also conclude that having a way to recognise and name the reflexive practices in play does help us to be aware of them, even when we are using memory and documentary traces to try to retrieve insights long after the study has been completed. Often the need to demonstrate and give an account of our research reflexivity becomes clear later in the study, after we have rushed ahead with the research and forgotten some of the usual good practices (such as keeping a research diary) that would provide the basis for a contemporaneous account. However, with an appropriate framework of reflexive practices to shape a retrospective description, it is possible to give an effective account of reflexivity in the research process, even if the benefits of a more informed, aware, and contemporaneous engagement have been missed.

I turn to the discussion of a collaborative research project in Chapter 6, where the intention was to maximise the authenticity and relevance of the research account, with generalisability approached more tentatively through theorisation. The focal study was the most recent (at the time of writing) in a series of studies using a specific, relationally reflexive approach (Hibbert, Sillince, Diefenbach & Cunliffe, 2014). I had worked for some time, with a group of friends, using a collaborative autoethnographic approach that allowed us to take roles as both researchers and participants. This approach allowed us to use our own experiences as the basis of research, and to be able to account for those experiences intimately on all reflexive levels – embodied, emotional, rational and relational – and so to be fully present in the study with significant control over our authentic voices.

The focal project in Chapter 6 arose from caring conversation within the group of friends, discussing the impact of negative emotional experiences on us during our academic careers. We felt that was a potentially useful topic for a research study that could focus on challenges for learning and leadership when facing such challenging emotional experiences, and that, based on wider conversations, the characterisations of these challenges and insights and ideas about how to address them could resonate with others. I focus on this study for two main reasons. The first reason is that it provides a contrast to the isolated, liminal and disempowered condition of doctoral research explored in Chapter 5. As a group of established academic staff, we had considerable freedom to decide what topics were of interest to us, and how to go about researching them. While relatively unusual approaches carry more risk when it comes to seeking publication, at our established career stages we could accommodate some risks within our portfolio. Our approach might be a more difficult 'sell' to a doctoral supervisor or committee in some contexts, although there are an increasing number of research groups and schools that accommodate this kind of work. The second and main reason for focussing on a collaborative autoethnographic project in Chapter 6 is that it provides a case in which reflexive practice was 'baked in' or intrinsic to the progress of the research. It would not have been possible to present authentic, resonant accounts as the basis of our insights if the group did not have both a good understanding of reflexivity and a commitment to reflexive practice.

The conclusions reached from the examination of a collaborative autoethnography in Chapter 6 focus on the influence of a commitment to a relationally reflexive method. That commitment led us to enlarge our circle of relational reflexive practice to incorporate external voices, and value internal voices in new ways. Published authors, engaged through their texts, were treated as trusted partners from whom we could actively receive ideas, along with critical voices that challenged our horizons of understanding. The internal conversation in our group provided a generative space for reflexive practice, helping us to operationalise our approach and record it authentically.

Across both case studies, in Chapters 5 and 6, there were also some common lessons and a number of other detailed insights. These chapters also provided the basis for re-approaching the theoretical material in the earlier chapters, in order to identify some of the key principles for 'how to be a reflexive researcher', while also identifying some opportunities for further work.

1.6   INTEGRATION: ANSWERING SOME QUESTIONS, RAISING NEW ISSUES

In Chapter 7, the concluding chapter of this book, I set out the key points that I have derived from my engagement with theory and experience in the realms of reflexivity and reflexive practice. In this section of the introduction, I therefore offer a summary of some of the main points set out in that chapter.

I conclude that the approach to reflexive practice that I develop is similar to established approaches, but self-reflexivity is given the primary position. It is from that perspective that other kinds of reflexivity are considered, through looking *at the self* (embodied and emotional reflexive practice) and looking *from the self* (rational and relational reflexive practice) to support critical engagement. I argue that this does not lead to an instrumental approach. Instead, it leads to an acceptance that we can go on, aware of our incompleteness and constraints but still struggling against these limits, without descending into a spiral of doubt that comes from radical reflexivity (Cunliffe, 2003; Cutcher, Hardy, Riach & Thomas, 2020).

In addition, I argue that my approach is also novel in its focus on time, through establishing the differences and connections between everyday future-oriented, adaptive reflexivity and the past-oriented, re-interpretive approach to reflexivity often associated with research projects. Bearing those temporal forms in mind, being a reflexive researcher entails understanding both the inevitably of reflexivity in our adaptation to experience and the choices we make (Archer, 2007), together with the possibilities for a greater degree of awareness in our reflexive practice. Those understandings also allow us to consider how more deliberate and aware forms of reflexive practice are accommodated (perhaps within groups) and how reflexive insights are captured (through simple tools such as research diaries and notes). However, the case studies (Chapters 5 and 6) also show that even if our awareness of reflexive practice is less than ideal during a study – and there may be many reasons for that – then it is possible to recover some insights much later, especially when intense emotional perceptions anchor our experiences (Hibbert,

Beech, Callagher & Siedlok, 2021). It is important, though, not to suggest that we can strip away interpretations in this way and get back to the 'facts' in past research projects. The facts (if there are such) are always at an unapproachable distance; it is interpretation all the way down (Gadamer, 1998; Hibbert & Huxham, 2010, 2011). However, a return to reflexive practice after the events can suggest other interpretations than those reached at the time, which may feel more authentic to ourselves and others. Overall, I argue for an integrated perspective on reflexive practice that brings embodied, emotional, rational and relational levels into a pattern moving between the future and the past, asking "*what I should do next?*" in the moments and months of our studies, while also asking "*how did I come to make those choices?*", in some cases long after the research has been concluded. This dual perspective brings everyday life and research practice into the same frame, constituting a scholarly way of life.

It is to be expected that a study of reflexive practice will lead to new issues and opportunities. You will be likely to form your own opinion on the questions that have arisen as you engage with this book from earlier chapters, but my personal perspective suggests two areas that present interesting opportunities for further study: the impact of personal health challenges on reflexive practice; and how reflexive practice is affected by institutional constraints.

A key example of personal health challenge that I focus on in Chapter 7 is mental health, and in particular anxiety and depression. This is an important and timely focus, given the long-established mental health crisis (Ehrenberg, 2009) and evidence of a particular problem in academia (Gorczynski, 2018). In addition to which, these are the health challenges with which I am most familiar and can connect with most authentically. Like any medical conditions, anxiety and depression impact on the practicalities and risks of conducting a study, but can also provide challenges in relation to what scholarly communities can accept as *legitimately felt* in the process of research and allow to be *authentically recorded* in a reflexive account (Todd, 2020).

A consideration of situational pressures and institutional constraints that have an effect on the possibilities for reflexive practice connects with approaches to critical reflexivity (see Chapter 2). A critically reflexive perspective focusses on the social constructions of tradition and ideology that shape our interpretive practice, in order to challenge the unquestioned norms that we reproduce in this way (Aronowitz, Deener, Keene, Schnittker & Tach, 2015; Hibbert, Beech & Siedlok, 2017; Hibbert, Coupland & MacIntosh, 2010; Hibbert & Huxham, 2010, 2011). I connect such objectives with engagement in rational and relational reflexive practice. This engagement helps to highlight how power differentials limit the disempowered person's ability to *say* what they experience through critical engagement and also undermine the empowered person's ability to *see* what the critical lens might reveal.

My overall conclusion, having staked a claim to contribute to ongoing debates, is that the answer to 'how to be a reflexive researcher' involves: taking a theoretical position; becoming familiar with reflexive practices; developing honesty about our abilities and constraints; and being responsible. In the chapters that follow, I hope to lead you to the same conclusion; or at least, for us to end up within the same shared horizon of understanding, where relational reflexive practice can help us both to learn when opportunities arise.

Dialogue

Each chapter of this book ends with a direct invitation to you, usually through questions that mirror how I would start a conversation about the ideas discussed. Some readers find this helpful, but it is not essential to the flow of the book. For now:

1. I open each chapter with a personal reflection, sometimes serious and sometimes less so. I think it is necessary to reveal something of yourself in order to discuss reflexivity authentically. What are your views about that?

2. I argue that a scholarly way of life brings everyday reflexive practice and reflexivity in research studies into the same frame. How does this relate to your experience, and with what consequences?

2. Reflexivity and research reflexivity

At one point during the early part of my doctoral studies, I felt that I was becoming obsessed with theory and philosophy. All of my reading was focussed on wrestling with the philosophical position underlying my methodology... after realising there was no agreement about any of this stuff in the field, with different authors outlining the three possible paradigms, or the seven, or the nine... and so on.

*I decided to wander to the bookstore to pick up some light reading, to take a break from the headache-inducing philosophical debate. Maybe I would grab a magazine, something trivial and ephemeral, I mused. Instead, I came back with a copy of **Philosophy Now**, which was probably a reflection of how I was both frustrated and fascinated at the same time...*

2.1 IS REFLEXIVITY A PHILOSOPHICAL PROJECT?

In the introductory chapter I described reflexivity as a "...a process of engaging with experience, that changes our ways of understanding and guides adaptation in readiness for future experiences". There are some 'big ticket' questions that can be unpacked within that statement, concerned with ideas about our being and becoming (what it means to be a person and how that is affected by adaptation and change) and the nature of understanding (how we come to know). Thinking about those questions can take us into very extensive philosophical debates about ontology and epistemology, but that is not the purpose of this book. So instead, I am going to address philosophical background questions very briefly, before moving on to a more direct focus on reflexivity as it is discussed in the context of everyday life and research practice.

Vu and Burton (2020) describe the terrain of philosophical foundations of reflexivity as including approaches based on a realist ontology and either a positivist epistemology or subjectivist epistemology. They allow for an underlying reality behind the phenomenon of reflexivity, but our means of understanding it – depending on the camp we find ourselves situated within – may claim to deliver an objectively true account or render insights that are unavoidably tied to subjective experience. These two positions differ in the degree of agency an individual has to see and challenge the situations which they find themselves in. However, in both cases reflexivity is about the choices people have, in relation to the objective circumstances that affect them (Archer, 2007), however they are understood.

In contrast, social constructionist writers, such as Nicholls (2009) and Parker, Racz and Palmer (2020), move away from personal choice and argue that reflexivity is not (or not only) an individual-level process. Instead, they emphasise how reflexivity is constituted and enabled in collective contexts through practices (Sklaveniti & Steyaert, 2020), in discourse (Collien, 2018), or in social institutions (Gray, 2008) that we nevertheless struggle to gain critical distance from. Those adopting a relational ontology, focussing on what is constructed or has its being *between* people in their everyday interaction, take a similar view (Rhodes & Carlsen, 2018; Allen, 2017). However, they focus on the positive, creative and generative nature of relational contexts, rather than addressing the struggle to escape their constraints. In consequence, they also tend to dwell on the moral consequences of a need to engage with others in ways that recognise essential intersubjective connections, bringing another layer of philosophy into view.

The approaches set out above lead to a focus on reflexivity as a concern for self-knowledge and change. They offer different ways of understanding the self and how action is constrained by that understanding, privileging either the importance of the internal conversation (Archer, 2007) or dialogue with others (Iszatt-White, Kempster & Carroll, 2017; Rhodes & Carlsen, 2018) as the basis of constituting ourselves and self-knowledge. The existence of positions with such different ontological and epistemological commitments means that the concepts these different views focus on will be contested (Mikkelsen & Clegg, 2019).

The existence of contested positions can, however, be accommodated within an instrumental approach that takes the view that "the reflexive researcher uses a set of practices involving the juxtaposition of perspectives to draw attention to the limitations in using a single frame of reference and, in so doing, provide new insights" (Alvesson, Hardy & Harley, 2008, p. 483). That kind of position requires an interpretivist perspective, in order to bring together difference kinds of insight within a coherent integrative frame. Burkitt (2012) also follows this interpretivist line, but for different reasons. He argues that in reflexivity:

> ...*we seek to interpret the meaning imputed to our actions, or to ourselves, by others with whom we are interrelated, or we seek to interpret the enigmatic aspects of ourselves.* (Burkitt, 2012, p. 464)

This view aligns with philosophical hermeneutic positions that argue that interpretation is not just a way of processing what we are seeking to bring to knowledge; instead, interpretation is seen to be intrinsic to the nature of knowing (Gadamer, 1998). This approach is not concerned with objective ontological assurances, and instead sees interpretation as our fundamental way of being in the world. We work within the constraints of our formative history and traditions that inform the unavoidable practice of interpretation as we go on with everyday life (Hibbert, Beech & Siedlok, 2017) and seek to be reflexive in relation to our experiences (Hibbert, Beech, Callagher & Siedlok, 2021; Hibbert, Callagher, Siedlok, Windahl & Kim, 2019). That is a good start for considering how scholars have interpreted and operationalised the idea of reflexivity, from their various viewpoints. Accordingly, in the remainder of this chapter I move on from philosophical debates to consider the ways in which reflexivity is discussed and applied, with reference to conceptualisations of everyday reflexivity and research reflexivity and the relationship between those areas of application. From there, I develop new characterisations of how reflexivity is enacted with a focus on either the future or the past, which have implications for both research practice and individual development.

2.2   TYPES OF REFLEXIVITY

Engaging with the topic of reflexivity is a complex task, not least because it has long been understood in a variety of ways (Holland, 1999), as the preceding discussion of philosophical approaches to the process has suggested. However, it is possible to organise the literature around a number of key themes, bearing in mind that other interpretations of the field will always be possible. Nevertheless, starting from some of the simplest concepts, that reflexivity is an adaptive process of thinking that changes how we think (Hibbert, Coupland & MacIntosh, 2010) or a process of engaging with experience that changes our ways of understanding and guides adaptation in readiness for future experiences, the main characterisations of reflexivity in the literature can be grouped under the following five themes:

Self-reflexivity, a process focussed on an individual's patterns of change and development, recursively linked to their ways of interpreting and living in the world (Archer, 2007; Caetano, 2017; Hibbert, Coupland & MacIntosh, 2010; Hibbert, Beech & Siedlok, 2017). This theme is focussed on the everyday processes of individual adaptation that are supported by reflexivity, which is considered to be an inescapable human activity (Archer, 2007). Importantly, while the focus of self-reflexivity is clearly on the individual, it can be understood from perspectives that focus on the individuals 'internal work' (Archer, 2007), or from viewpoints that look at how individuals change through interaction with others (Gilmore & Kenny, 2015), or from perspectives that include both of these alternatives (Hibbert, Beech, Callagher & Siedlok, 2021).

Critical reflexivity, an approach focussed on understanding how we come to interpret the world in the way that we do, through the social constructions of tradition and ideology (Aronowitz, Deener, Keene, Schnittker & Tach, 2015; Hibbert, Beech & Siedlok, 2017; Hibbert, Coupland & MacIntosh, 2010;

Hibbert & Huxham, 2010, 2011). Critical reflexivity stands in contrast to the (often unconscious) process of adaptation involved in self-reflexivity, since it seeks to interrupt and challenge the basis for interpreting and acting on our experience. Critical reflexivity can still, however, overlap with self-reflexivity in its effects since it involves:

> *...questioning our own assumptions and taken-for-granted actions, thinking about where/who we are and where/who we would like to be, challenging our conceptions of reality, and exploring new possibilities.* (Cunliffe, 2004, p. 411)

Relational reflexivity, which considers how an individual's patterns of change and development in their ways of interpreting and living in the world are influenced and shaped through ongoing social relationships (Hibbert, Sillince, Diefenbach & Cunliffe, 2014; Cutcher, Hardy, Riach & Thomas, 2020). This theme considers the interdependence of individuals in social contexts and the ways in which our thinking is shaped by the influence and insights of others, and how we influence them in turn. Conceptualisations overlap with critical reflexivity in some ways, but as well as highlighting the challenge that comes from entertaining alternative viewpoints, relational reflexivity entails a willingness to move into liminal, in-between spaces and engage with what emerges within them (Nicholls, 2009). This involves curiosity about the other, openness to the possibility of learning with them and a willingness to engage in generative dialogue rather than limited critical discussion (Chilvers & Kearnes, 2020; Hibbert, Siedlok & Beech, 2016; Rhodes & Carlsen, 2018).

Radical reflexivity, which takes the principles of self- and critical reflexivity to their ultimate conclusion by denying robust foundational truths or easily generalisable insights about how we live in and interpret the world, in favour of local, subjective explanations (Allen, Cunliffe & Easterby-Smith, 2019; Cunliffe, 2003; Pollner, 1991). It is a difficult process to engage with, in the context of research, since it involves difficult questions that introduce doubt and are never fully resolved:

> *How to be here and there (in the [practitioner's] setting/experience/language/emotions and the academic's setting/experience/language/emotions)?*
> *How to be here, there and in between (how to span the boundaries between those worlds, between theory and practice, between different language games, to develop accounts plausible to both? How can I become 'involved', yet record 'data'? Can I interpret, explain, just present dialogue as collaborative sense making in the moment, draw conclusions...)?*
> *How to avoid being believed too much (this is the absolute truth) or too little (this is too trivial, local, convoluted... to be convincing)?* (Cunliffe, 2003, p. 998)

Radical reflexivity therefore leads to the consideration of multiple interpretations of our experience and possibilities for action, with criteria for judgement between interpretations based on local and temporary intersubjective consensus.

Instrumental reflexivity, which provides a balance or contrast to radical reflexivity by using the principles of critical reflexivity in a constrained and focussed approach, to remove less robust or persuasive insights about how we live in and interpret the world (Weick, 1999) or assemble a different critical view on the world or focal phenomenon through the thoughtful combination of insights from a range of perspectives (Alvesson, Hardy & Harley, 2008). Instrumental reflexivity is a pragmatic approach to avoiding an endless spiral of doubt, with the trade-off that it can lead us to be unaware of the unquestioned foundational ideas on which we stand (for example, commitment to a particular paradigm: Cunliffe, 2011; Deetz, 1996).

In addition to the differences that are set out in the categorisations above, there are also key differences in terms of the kinds of focus adopted in different parts of the literature. Some treatments are more concerned with reflexivity per se, as it is experienced in everyday life, while others are interested in reflexivity as a process in (especially interpretive) research (Hibbert, Coupland & MacIntosh, 2010). However, it is sometimes difficult to separate the treatments since reflexivity, as a process of adaptation, shows that all individuals – whether engaged in research or not – modify their understandings and interactions in response to their interpretation of their experience, but face constraints as they do so (Hibbert, Beech & Siedlok, 2017). Thus, self-reflexivity, to be engaged with in a more deliberate way, needs to connect with critical, relational or radical reflexive approaches. In other words, we need to be aware that we are not neutral observers nor detached from the contexts that we seek to study; we all bring something of ourselves, which we have not fully explored, to the research context and that will shape how we understand our experience within it (Caetano, 2017; Hibbert, Coupland & MacIntosh, 2010). For some, this is what *research* reflexivity seeks to overcome, or at least mitigate.

Alternative Approaches to Implementing Research Reflexivity

Researchers appropriate the process of adaptation at the heart of reflexivity to focus on it in one of two ways. Those seeking to produce an objective account turn the process of reflexivity more deliberately on themselves and their understandings with the aim of correcting the bias (Weick, 1999) that comes from their own situatedness, and so seek to produce (more) generalisable insights. However, an alternative appropriation foregrounds and inhabits the process of adaptation in response to experience, instead of trying to cut back to an underlying reality. Those taking the alternative, social constructionist approach focus on the learning *in that process* and *within the specific context*, in order to give an account that may resonate with the experience of others

(Cunliffe, 2003; Hibbert, Sillince, Diefenbach & Cunliffe, 2014). This alternative approach pays more attention to the uniqueness of individual human experience and, recognising the limits of objectivity, strives instead to generate an authentic subjective understanding (Cunliffe, 2003, 2004, 2011). Given these alternatives, how researchers understand and apply reflexivity usually depends on their ontological and epistemological commitments, the aims of their study, and the claims they wish to make.

I follow the interpretivist approach (as discussed earlier) and see either positivist or social constructionist positions as ways of interpreting experience within a particular tradition. With that in mind, and allowing for the five themes presented earlier and both approaches to research to be incorporated, reflexivity and research reflexivity can be formally defined as follows:

Reflexivity is the process by which individuals, interpreting their experience from within their situated tradition, come to understand their social context and relationships with others and use this understanding to adapt themselves and their personal projects.

Research reflexivity is the process by which researchers, interpreting their experience of research from within their situated tradition, seek to be aware of the process of learning and adaptation and foreground their situatedness, in order to achieve one of two aims:

(i)   Maximise the *generalisability* of the understandings generated in their research projects, by eliminating the influence of their situated interpretive stance, as much as that is possible.
(ii) Maximise the *authenticity* and *resonance* of the understandings generated in their research projects, through drawing attention to and building on the richness of their situated interpretive stance, as much as that is possible.

Research Reflexivity in Interpretive Research

Both generalisability and authenticity/resonance approaches to research reflexivity can be applied in the context of interpretive research. The differences in the dynamics of these two approaches are clearest in modes where interaction with research participants is open and unstructured: namely, ethnographic field research.

Field research can include autoethnographic studies in which the researcher's personal experience is key to generating authentic and resonant research accounts (Boncori & Smith, 2019; Davies, McGregor & Horan, 2019; Fernando, Reveley & Learmonth, 2020). However, field research most often involves the collection of original data of multiple forms in social or organisational settings. This usually includes (inter alia) observational material or insights from participant observation (Edmondson & McManus, 2007; Peticca-Harris, deGama & Elias, 2016; Vinten, 1994), within a loose study framework. That kind of loose framework challenges researchers to consider their biases in relation to what is recognised (or not) as useful data (Galibert, 2004), as well as problematising how data should be collected and interpreted in ways that reflect participant understandings (Gioia, Corley & Hamilton, 2012; Okumus, Altinay & Roper, 2007). Such approaches seek to focus on robustness and generalisability through stripping away the researchers' unchallenged interpretations. Field research therefore provides a suitable context to consider how research reflexivity of either of the kinds described earlier is enacted, since studies of both kinds are well established. Considering how both generalisability-focussed and authenticity-focussed approaches play out in field research settings leads to the identification of two orientations of reflexivity, which highlight some of the key links between everyday and research reflexivity in practice.

The first theme comes into view by thinking about autoethnographic research approaches. Such approaches depend, at least in part, on capturing how reflexivity is used to adapt to our environments and change our research practice, alongside our way of being with others that feature in our situated contexts (Beech, Hibbert, McInnes & MacIntosh, 2009). Our focus is on others through their effect on us. With this focus, it is possible to bring together insights focussed on self- and relational reflexivity (Archer, 2007; Cutcher, Hardy, Riach & Thomas, 2020; Hibbert, Coupland & MacIntosh, 2010; Hibbert, Sillince, Diefenbach & Cunliffe, 2014). This entails both a concern for our own future as well as how we are engaging with others in order to make that future possible. The integrated approach under this theme can therefore be characterised as *future-oriented reflexivity*. This orientation is focussed on the ways in which reflexivity is involved in how we *actively* change and develop, in response to the ways that we interpret our experience of the world, from moment to moment. In future-oriented reflexivity, change in the researcher's ways of being and doing are the most important outcomes.

Second, considering how field researchers seek to use reflexivity to look back on our research experiences, in order to challenge the biases involved in our interpretations, brings together insights focussed on instrumental reflexivity, critical reflexivity and radical reflexivity (Alvesson, Hardy & Harley, 2008; Cunliffe, 2003; Weick, 1999), all of which involve questioning how we have arrived at our interpretations. Taking these themes together brings a different process into view. Although instrumental, critical and radical approaches to reflexivity have different ontological and epistemological commitments and limits, they are all concerned with looking below the surface assumptions of *past* experience. That is, these themes are concerned with how social and historical contexts have shaped us without any deliberate action on our part (Cunliffe, 2004; Hibbert, Coupland & MacIntosh, 2010), leading us to arrive at each moment with preunderstandings that shape how we interpret the world (Gadamer, 1998). This kind of engagement with our interpretive and formative hinterland (Hibbert, Beech & Siedlok, 2017) can be characterised as *past-oriented reflexivity*.

The rest of this chapter focusses on characterising future-oriented and past-oriented reflexivity in more detail, in order to develop implications for research practice and researcher self-development. The argument proceeds in three main parts. First, future-oriented reflexivity is examined, as an inevitable process that yet entails a complex struggle, along with the key choices about how research practice is shaped moment-by-moment, that follow from thoughtful engagement with this process. Second, a more detailed picture of past-oriented reflexivity is developed, with insights for enhanced researcher self-understanding, learning and change, along with the key implications for research practice that flow from those possibilities. In the final section, future-oriented and past-oriented reflexivity are brought together, as an integrated approach that informs interpretive engagement in research practice and supports researcher self-development.

2.3   FUTURE-ORIENTED REFLEXIVITY: PROCESS AND STRUGGLE

Reflexivity as a Process of Adaptation

As discussed earlier, descriptions of reflexivity as a human process are numerous. However, all of the descriptions have at least a partial foundation in the idea that individuals can adapt, on a range of levels and through different processes, in response to their interpretation of experience (Archer, 2007; Caetano, 2017; Hibbert, Coupland & MacIntosh, 2010). Adaptations may take effect in a range of way, involving one or more of:

(i)   A change in understanding about something(s) and/or person(s) in our social context, so that we think differently about that (kind of) situation.
(ii)   A change in our patterns of interaction with other individuals in the social context, to better reflect a new understanding.
(iii) A change in the way we understand and develop ourselves as individuals in order to support purposive choices – about our way of life, our personal projects, or even our survival – in a given context.

As researchers, it is important to understand these processes of adaptation, which are usually overlapping, if we are going to use reflexivity to make our research projects more authentic and robust. This is because we are always *already* reflexive, always *already* involved in and changing in response to our interpretation of the research contexts that we are trying to be objective about (Hibbert, Coupland & MacIntosh, 2010). Thus, future-oriented reflexivity can be characterised as an inevitable process, which we need in some way to 'keep up with'.

While the process is inevitable, that does not mean that we *do* always 'keep up with it' or are even fully aware of it. This is because we are shaped by our social context in ways that we normally leave unquestioned, and inhabit those contexts as embodied, physically engaged beings (Eriksen, Van Echo, Harmel, Kane, Curran, Gustafson & Shults, 2005; Schmutz, Lei, Eppich & Manser, 2018). Rather than being isolated and unchanging rational intellects, we arrive at every situation shaped by past experiences. The formational effects of experience begin to take a hold of us before we can really have any choice in the matter. In particular, we are shaped by language acquisition, cultural norms and early educational experiences about which we have had little or no choice; through such formational experiences we are shaped to understand from within particular traditions (Caetano, 2017; Gadamer, 1998; Hibbert & Huxham, 2010; Hibbert, Siedlok & Beech, 2016; Mahdevan, 2015).

As embodied beings our interpretations are also in dialogue with our physicality in numerous ways. I am not focussing (at this point) on the various ways in which our physicality is received and responded to in social contexts, but instead am concerned with insights from biological and medical science that we may not always consider. Such insights include (for example) the operations and effects of our hormonal systems (Hardy & Hibbert, 2012) and internal bodily signals (Tsakiris & De Preester, 2019) on our behaviours, and the effects of our physical and mental health (Aronowitz, Deener, Keene, Schnittker & Tach, 2015; Todd, 2020) on how we interpret our experiences. In addition, working with and between the influence of social context and our physicality are a range of emotional dynamics (Immordino-Yang, 2016; Quadt, Critchley & Garfinkel, 2019) which also influence the processes of reflexive adaptation (Hibbert, Beech, Callagher & Siedlok, 2021; Hibbert, Callagher, Siedlok, Windahl & Kim, 2019).

All of the levels of influence – social/traditional, physical, and emotional – on reflexivity are important. They lead to the conclusion that, while reflexivity is inevitable, making it a really *conscious* process that we are able to *direct* is a complex struggle and only ever a partial success. Unless we make a choice to engage in deliberate reflexive practice, even that partial success is not possible. In everyday life, we are not usually 'in charge' of how we interpret what we experience, nor do we deliberately plan how experience will change us. As

Bourdieu (2004, p. 115) put it, "I know that I am caught up and comprehended in the world that I take as my object."

Choosing to Adapt in the Process of Research

If we are seeking to be deliberately reflexive, we have to attend to our own adaptation in the research context as we seek to navigate the way *forward* in completing our study. These choices will have a strong, shaping influence on the kind of material we have for past-oriented reflexivity to work on, which we can question and unpack in more depth at a later time. The primary choice that we can make is about which of two research reflexivity approaches we will adopt. As noted earlier, that is a choice between these two options:

(i)   Maximise the *generalisability* of the understandings generated in our research projects, by eliminating the influence of our situated interpretive stance, as much as that is possible.
(ii) Maximise the *authenticity* and *resonance* of the understandings generated in our research projects, through drawing attention to and building on the richness of our situated interpretive stance, as much as that is possible.

At this point, to illustrate the different forms of account and kinds of insight that are developed through commitment to each of these alternative positions on reflexivity, I offer an empirical example from my own experience. To show the implications of following each of the alternatives, two accounts – one generalisability focussed and one authenticity focussed – of experience in a particular context are offered, which are labelled as the *HouseCo* example. This is a pseudonym for a large international company producing consumer goods. The experience that is explored relates to my participant observation in one of the company's sites in the United Kingdom. The focus of this (unpublished) research eventually became centred on diversity and discrimination. The brief accounts set out below are adapted to preserve anonymity, in the normal way.

An account focussed on applying research reflexivity for generalisability:

I was aware that as a white person of UK descent, I was part of the overwhelming majority at *HouseCo*. At a site employing around several hundred people, the number of people of non-European descent was in single figures, and accents suggesting that individuals came from outside the UK were similarly rare in my encounters on site. This lack of diversity was similar to the region in which *HouseCo* was situated.

Early on, I thought that this near mono-cultural context meant that I might be unlikely to observe any action or talk related to discrimination, over time I realised that I was looking for diversity in a way that was conditioned by my experience in a more cosmopolitan part of the UK. The differences that were commented on by people at *HouseCo* focussed on origins from other parts of the UK, especially people from the South of England, who were occasionally ridiculed. However, since it was possible that my own inter-actions as an obvious 'Southerner' could be stimulating some of this talk, I could instead focus on observations of some other dynamics where my presence is not a 'confounding factor'.

An account focussed on applying research reflexivity for authenticity and resonance:

On arrival at *HouseCo* I had soon noticed the casual sexist and homophobic remarks that seemed not to shock the other workers. For example, referring to gay men as "benders" was the usual term (used by both men and women), although there were quite a few other offensive terms and nobody seemed surprised. This reminded me of my childhood rather than my recent adult experience; it was a kind of talk that seemed both unpleasant and dated – although that interpretation may have reflected my more recent experience in an intellectual environment pretty far from my working-class roots.

I was not – am not – very obvious as a gay man, and my orientation was not questioned. In any case, childhood experiences had taught me how to avoid scrutiny without lying if I wished, and I just wanted to fit in. Although I'd had enough experience of it, I was not sure whether the homophobic talk in this case was a cultural legacy, or whether there was some current engine of hate within it. It was not as though people knew that someone gay was in the room when they made the remarks that I noted, so maybe there was no explicit intent to cause harm. However, on one occasion I was chatting with 'Dave' during a lunch break and he mentioned a TV program that had unexpectedly featured gay characters. Presuming I would agree, he said, "It's bloody disgusting, isn't it?" I was beginning to feel that I'd soaked up enough of this stuff, so I said, "I don't agree Dave. I'm gay, so no, I don't think it's disgusting." Dave's face was contorted with revulsion as he instantly responded, "People like you should be fucking shot."

Table 2.1   *Future-oriented research reflexivity approaches: the HouseCo example*

Adaptive process	Research reflexivity approach favouring:	
	Generalisability	*Authenticity & resonance*
A change in understanding about something(s) and/or person(s) in our social context, so that we think differently about that context.	A realisation that the apparent homogeneity of the context was illusionary, and that variations of different kinds than presumed were noted.	The discovery that 'dated' homophobic language was not symptomatic of a cultural legacy, but associated with active hate.
A change in our patterns of interaction with other individuals in the social context, to better reflect a new understanding.	A newly situated awareness of one's own 'otherness' leads to a determination to set aside talk focussed on that otherness and consider 'neutral' themes.	A focal incident both revealed an existing separation and reinforced it; personal otherness was brought to centre stage in the account.
A change in the way we understand and develop ourselves as an individual in order to support purposive choices – about our way of life, our personal projects, or even our survival – in a given context.	A realisation that looking for evidence of diversity in certain ways itself reflects cultural conditioning, and that there is a need to be open to alternate understandings.	The discovery of active homophobic hate led to a determination to be politically engaged and open, but also to be more self-aware about the dangers of the context.

Learning and Changing Through Research Reflexivity

The difference in the two approaches outlined above is obvious. It is also clear that *both* approaches can be applied in a given research situation to some extent, but eventually there has to be a commitment to focus on either writing yourself *out* of the account or writing yourself *in*. However, both approaches also demonstrate (or at least lead to the possibility of) future-oriented adaptation in the process of reflexivity. The choice of research stance towards either neutral generalisability or involved authenticity leads to two different outcomes, although the application of each stance can described using the same adaptive process steps: (i) A change in understanding about something(s) and/or person(s) leading us to think differently about our context; (ii) A change in our patterns of interaction with other individuals, to better reflect a new understanding; and (iii) A change in the way we understand and develop ourselves as an individual in order to support purposive choices. To illustrate the variations in outcome, the approaches are compared in Table 2.1.

There are two key implications to note from the points made in Table 2.1. The first is that, for either approach to research reflexivity, the individual involved in the reflexive process is learning and changing during the fieldwork, rather than simply collecting data. Thus, in the case of *either* approach to research reflexivity, altered personal understandings of the focal social context and relational dynamics will open up new ways of seeing and engaging inside and outside of the research situation. This means that learning from reflexive research is never confined to the formal insights from analysis of the study material. Instead, the learning that is experienced, especially if recognised during the process of research, will shape the development of the fieldwork and *also* change the researcher, unless the area of study is somehow of no *personal* relevance or interest to them. It is, however, difficult to imagine anyone committing to the intensive work involved in interpretive research in the field, and the patient processes of interpretive analysis, if the project is focussed on something about which they care little. Why would anyone choose to do that? Even the most rarefied scholarly interest in a project will involve some personal investment in how the resultant work will be received.

The second implication that follows, from the points outlined in Table 2.1, is that there is an evident critical engagement (Aronowitz, Deener, Keene, Schnittker & Tach, 2015; Hibbert, 2013) in the way in which my experiences have been recorded and reflected upon. This critical engagement underlines my personal situatedness in a tradition that values diversity and equality, but also my own prejudices and assumptions about what these values mean in the given context. Recognising the assumptions motivating our critique is an important counterpart to an individually focussed understanding of reflexivity, by looking at the process by which our understanding of, and engagement in, the social world is shaped. Bringing that process into the foreground opens up the possibility of critique in another dimension, in relation to the otherwise uncontested assumptions delivered to us through our formation over time (Caetano, 2017; Gadamer, 1998; Hibbert, Beech & Siedlok, 2017), that cause us to interpret the world in certain ways. This turns the focus away from *future* development, new understandings and change to consider the foundations of our interpretive approach which lie in the *past*.

2.4   PAST-ORIENTED REFLEXIVITY: UNDERSTANDING AND CHANGE

While future-oriented reflexivity can be unconscious or deliberate, past-oriented reflexivity can only be a deliberate choice, whether close to the moment of experience or in much later recollection. As such, engagement in past-oriented reflexivity involves three processes that can take place in the context of experience or in later reflexive processes (such as writing):

(i)   Recognising that our own traditional and ideological formation shapes our initial interpretations (Hibbert, Beech & Siedlok, 2017; Shils, 1981), and deciding how we signify that formation.

(ii)   Recognising who is privileged (and who is excluded or diminished) in a given context, how that relates to the norms of our own cultural traditions (Namatende-Sakwa, 2018), and considering the alternative choices that are opened up by that recognition.

(iii) Recognising how our practice may sustain and perpetuate the traditional positions and ideologies which were intrinsic to our own formation, and deciding whether and how we should interrupt our role in this process of perpetuation to connect with the understandings of others (Hibbert, Sillince, Diefenbach & Cunliffe, 2014).

Formation and the Limits of Reflexivity

All individuals interpret through tradition (Gadamer, 1998; Hibbert, Beech & Siedlok, 2017); it is not necessary to have an overt commitment to an historically rooted community for our patterns of understanding to be shaped by our past. None of us chose where and among whom we would be born and raised. Our formation in a particular time and place gives us a way of understanding that we usually apply by default, without having to consciously decide to do so (Hibbert & Huxham, 2010, 2011).

Thus, our interpretations always come from somewhere and there is no such thing as a 'neutral' perspective. To see something is to see it *as* something. This pre-given aspect of how we interpret what we experience was described by Vandevelde (2010) as the 'vertical' aspect of interpretation; there is something laid down in our past, on which our interpretations build. These foundational interpretations serve as normative assumptions, until we see that there are other ways of interpreting when we are disturbed by challenging experiences (Hibbert, Callagher, Siedlok, Windahl & Kim, 2019) or open conversation with others. That is, looking and listening at the world around us leads to what Vandevelde (2010) calls the 'horizontal' aspect of interpretation – the alternative understandings that can exist in parallel at any given time, shaped by different 'vertical communities' (socio-historical groupings), and how our initial interpretations are confirmed or contested by these other possibilities.

Past-oriented reflexivity uses the horizontal aspect of interpretation – recognising that there are multiple ways of interpreting at any given time – to suggest that all have particular 'roots' and so we cannot assume that our own foundations are more solid than the alternatives. In doing so, past-oriented reflexivity seeks to explicate and question the foundational traditions that shape our current and future interpretations (Davey, 2006, 2013; Fairfield, 2011; Gadamer, 1998; Grondin, 2011; Hibbert, Beech & Siedlok, 2017), and to cautiously apply the same questioning approach to those around us (in personal as well as research contexts). Think, for example, of the different political and legal traditions that we regard as providing a legitimate framework of control for our daily lives, the religious and cultural traditions that have influenced gender roles in societies, and the ways that the languages in which we think can favour certain kinds of thought patterns above others (Epstein, 2016). Thus, it should be no surprise that, say, an atheist living in Sweden, a Christian living in the United States and a Muslim in Saudi Arabia might all understand and interpret the world differently. All of us have ways of interpreting the world that we inhabit, as well as constraints about how clearly and 'objectively' we can understand ourselves, that have been shaped by a formative context and process that was both unchosen and inherently subjective (Hibbert, Beech & Siedlok, 2017).

Importantly, in everyday life we are under no obligation to 'unpack' our assumptions or excavate their historical roots; in addition, arguably, this would often feel unnecessary. To take some trivial examples: it is not important to know how and why national cuisines developed as they did when you choose your lunch, nor is it necessary to understand the roots of the English language when you say "hello" to someone on the street. While it could be interesting to answer these questions, we don't need to do so to carry on daily life. Our formative past, understood in this way, is a practical and convenient process of being shaped by tradition, reflecting the cultural norms our communities have inherited and passed on to us as practical tools for everyday life. Indeed, tradition's convenience (and therefore its endurance) lies in serving up easy answers for how to go about everyday life (Davey 2006, 2011, 2013), answers that have worked well enough in the past that there is no obvious need to examine them (Gadamer, 1998; Hibbert & Huxham, 2010, 2011; Shils, 1981).

Arguably then, for most of us and for most of the time, we have no need to look into the roots of our thinking; it is not necessary for going on with everyday life, and it could introduce doubt and contradiction that might be unwelcome (Archer, 2007; Cunliffe & Jun, 2005; Hibbert, Siedlok & Beech, 2016), through uncovering reasons to change our approach that we might otherwise not encounter. A need to change our approach, however compelling the reasons for it, is thus not necessarily welcome and may be resisted because it can undermine the solidity of our sense of self; for that reason, while it might be a rational response to past-oriented reflexivity, it can be tangled up with difficult emotions that work against it (Hibbert, Callagher, Siedlok, Windahl & Kim, 2019). So, if we return to future-oriented reflexivity for a moment, while this is a universal and inalienable human activity (Archer, 2007), it often uses the tools offered up by tradition to craft a way forward (Hibbert & Huxham, 2010; Shils, 1981). While the tools of tradition are in use and working effectively, they are rarely examined. For that reason, past-oriented reflexivity is, in contrast to future-oriented reflexivity, *not* a universal human activity and needs to be engaged with deliberately, particularly in research studies. That does not mean, however, that we always choose when and how to take this deliberate step.

Triggered Reflexivity and Alternative Choices

In addition to deliberate applications (for example, in research studies) there is also an unpredictable and somewhat unintentional route into past-oriented reflexivity. It can be triggered by an impression that something is not quite right, that the interpretations which we would normally use to pilot a way forward are suddenly open to question. This feeling of radical doubt is not necessarily (or at least not immediately) rational; instead, it can involve emotional or even visceral sensations of being unsettled and ill-at-home in some situation (Hardy & Hibbert, 2012; Hibbert, Callagher, Siedlok, Windahl & Kim, 2019). Cunliffe (2003, 2004) describes this kind of experience of realising something is not right as 'being struck'; the result is that what was once certain is now troublesome and demands both critical inquiry and personal introspection.

While visceral and emotional reactions (Hardy & Hibbert, 2012) accompany an experience of being struck that is sudden, similar experiences can occur which are different from that kind of instantaneous shock. There can be a slow dawning of awareness, developing alongside a growing and persistent sense of dissatisfaction with what we have – hitherto – interpreted as meaningful and valuable in our approach to life. For example, Archer (2007) describes individuals who have this experience of reflexivity as 'meta reflexives', who re-orient their lives towards a new vocation, for example through engagement with particular vocational, artistic or religious communities. This re-orientation hints at an important aspect of past-oriented reflexivity; it can require engagement with others to fully open up the possibilities for interpreting differently (Hibbert, Coupland & MacIntosh, 2010). Archer (2007) also describes other ways in which individuals experience and engage with reflexivity through the characterisation of three further reflexive types. One of these types is the 'fractured reflexive', whose internal conversations increase their discomfort with their present understanding of their place in the world, but do not lead to a new way forward. A path to change is also absent for 'communicative reflexives', who more-or-less unquestioningly accept the traditions of their current community and their place within it and for 'autonomous reflexives', who build on the traditions of their current community to seek material advancement on socially accepted standards. Archer's (2007) analysis powerfully illustrates how for many people, in the absence of challenging engagement in past-oriented reflexivity, future-oriented reflexivity can be directed towards stasis rather than finding an alternative way forward, even when that might be desirable on rational grounds (Archer, 2007; Caetano, 2017; Hibbert, Coupland & MacIntosh, 2010). The same construction and constraint is, of course, true for all of us. We all have different abilities and constraints that affect our possibilities for expression, in contexts where we come to understand and interpret the world in ways that do not fit with the assumptions of dominant cultures and ideologies. To understand how we can illuminate and express alternative possibilities, researchers need to explore the roots of preferred understandings and determine why we defend them.

Past-oriented Research Reflexivity in Practice: A Critical Project

Researchers can often feel surprised or disappointed by individuals whose form of reflexivity favours stasis and the status quo, especially when that may involve complicity in the construction of social norms that work to their disadvantage (Hibbert & Cunliffe, 2015; Mahdevan, 2015). It is a puzzle why individuals, for example, seem to trust political groups whose policies are likely to disadvantage them, and do not look behind the ideological assumptions driving a position in which flaws or doubts can easily be established (at least from an external perspective). The problem is that it can be difficult to draw a clear line between a harmful lack of scrutiny that has a clear impact on social outcomes, in contrast to more harmless and convenient everyday assumptions when the impact on individuals is not immediately obvious. For example, it might not matter why our greeting is "hello", but it might matter a great deal who we choose to say hello *to*, and who we choose to ignore (Callagher, El Sahn, Hibbert, Korber & Siedlok, 2021). The temptation in past-oriented research reflexivity is to press on with the imposition of our 'enlightened' value judgements about others in our descriptions of, and interaction with, the world... while our *own* everyday assumptions remain unexamined. We are always looking from a particular point of view; that cannot be avoided, but we need to know where we stand and why we do so. For that reason, when interpreting the choices of others, as researchers we need to think deeply about the traditions that inform our *own* subjective understandings and choices.

As briefly discussed earlier, deliberately working to understand the social construction of our own subjectivity often goes under the label 'critical reflexivity' (Aronowitz, Deener, Keene, Schnittker & Tach, 2015; Hibbert, Coupland & MacIntosh, 2010) since it exposes our linguistic, social and cultural 'taken-for-granteds' – our traditions – and seeks to open them up to critique (Hibbert & Huxham, 2010; Vandevelde, 2010). This is also a critical project in the sense that it reveals the power distributed by such 'taken-for-granted' assumptions, which produces winners and losers. As Archer's (2007) study of reflexivity in pivotal life choices shows, the socialised knowledge that shapes our interpretation of the world is often associated with ideologies that justify the status quo. Dominant ideologies are inherently partisan and motivated by particular interests; they protect the advantage of highly influential sectors of society and even determine which ways of understanding are valued (Deetz, 1996; Hibbert, Sillince, Diefenbach & Cunliffe, 2014; Jost & Hunyady, 2005; Rhodes, 2009; Stoddart, 2007). An ideological position is normally defended as logical by carefully delimiting the terms of debate that might otherwise be used to challenge it.

Think, for example, of the understandings of gender and social roles prevalent in different societies. Traditional interpretations have supported structural inequality against women in most of the world, for most of history; in many societies such understandings are changing slowly, but still leave their legacy of inequalities and tacit assumptions that affect women's lives and choices almost everywhere. In many societies, women are still clearly and radically limited, disempowered and disadvantaged in fundamental ways (Eriksen, Van Echo, Harmel, Kane, Curran, Gustafson & Shults, 2005; Mahdevan, 2015). The existence of both subtle and muscular forms of gender inequality is well established, but the jumping-off point for consideration of past-oriented reflexivity is *not* that such social conditions exist, but instead that they are somehow unconsidered and treated as normal (or normative), even if that is only by those who profit from inequality. Past-oriented, critical reflexivity should help to unsettle the sense of normality in such cases; it will reveal the patterns of understanding that otherwise remain unchallenged, along with our unexamined complicity in maintaining such patterns (Archer, 2007; Mahdevan, 2015). Working with a colleague in an earlier study (Hibbert & Cunliffe, 2015), I captured a good example of how past-oriented reflexivity can unsettle a sense of normality. Our article describes how the point of view of an engineering manager in a Middle East-based oil company was affected by an encounter with feminist critique (Bell, 2010), during a reflexive study:

> *Both my company and my tribe share a unique feature that women have secondary roles, they are not involved in general and public issues and their voices are barely heard. [My company] claim they support women's rights and encourage them to take active roles. Personally, I did not see that since the majority of the women are working as secretaries, receptionists, and nurses but almost no one is handling a critical leadership role. As a father of four girls, this brings many questions, what the future of my daughters will be, what type of life roles they will play, will they be active members of the society? This definitely causes me to spare no effort to educate them and give them [more] room to express their thoughts and ideas.*
> (Hibbert & Cunliffe, 2015, pp. 182–183)

In order to replace the structure of what we already know and see things differently, we need to take on a different, distanciated point of view from which to envision the old structure in order to pull it apart. It is not possible to generate an alternative and compelling point of view from benign introspection. Instead, we need to be persuaded to entertain a new and less familiar position from which things inevitably look different (Aronowitz, Deener, Keene, Schnittker & Tach, 2015; Hibbert, Sillince, Diefenbach & Cunliffe, 2014; Myers, 2010). Developing a different position in this way is not straightforward. It requires that some alternative perspective, some different frame of interpretation, is placed into *confrontation* with our comfortable position, consistent with Vandevelde's (2010) horizontal dimension of debate in interpretive processes. We stop standing on the (invisible) rock of our tradition and take a few steps to the side, from which point we can gain a view of where we were standing. But that involves *really* leaving our familiar position behind, at least for a while. For that reason, past-oriented research reflexivity requires engagement with others, whether directly through conversation or through indirect means of influence such as scholarly reading or engagement with art, that help us to see in a different way (Danchev, 2011; Hibbert, Sillince, Diefenbach & Cunliffe, 2014; Hibbert, Beech & Siedlok, 2017). Thus, an element of relational reflexivity is important to making past-oriented reflexivity truly effective.

Relational connections and insights can arise serendipitously. That is, sometimes alternative viewpoints may become evident in the context of our research, if we are engaging with participants collaboratively and on (as much as possible) a basis of equality (Cassell, Radcliffe & Malik, 2020; Hibbert, Sillince, Diefenbach & Cunliffe, 2014). Nevertheless, a difficult problem remains; the initial engagement with alternative viewpoints is, unavoidably, through our own traditionally informed interpretations. To continue the earlier metaphor, the new rocks we choose to step onto, from which to view our own rock, are those that look attractive from our comfortable position. In contrast, the process of letting go and/or temporarily taking *uncomfortable* alternative views seriously can be a struggle. However, those who do entertain alternative views effectively may find that it introduces a further problem – every viewpoint requires examination from another, such that the process is potentially limitless. There are always other alternative viewpoints, none is necessarily the 'right' approach and it is hard to justify any view as objectively foundational. This lack of any obvious endpoint to the critical examination, entailed in past-oriented reflexivity, can lead to a spiral of self-undermining uncertainty (Cunliffe, 2003). Thus, past-oriented research reflexivity requires openness to alternative viewpoints (and even the adoption of practices to actively seek these alternatives), but it needs to be combined with introspection to anchor interpretations in the researcher's (examined) values. In this way it is possible to arrive at provisional understandings that are good enough to 'go on'. Researchers need to take care not to enter into a spiral of *endless* doubt; this remains a possible and even 'valid' outcome of past-oriented research reflexivity, but it is pragmatically useless. Instead, as Marshall and Reason argue, it is necessary "…to see evocative evidence of the researcher as both alive and disciplined in the research account" (2007, p. 376).

Table 2.2   *Past-oriented research reflexivity approaches*

Critical process	Research reflexivity approach favouring:	
	Generalisability	*Authenticity & resonance*
Recognising that our own ideological formation shapes our initial interpretations in the field (including the fact that a critical position is *itself* ideological).	Support for objective, purely factual elements of observations must be close to data, with reflection on our own position used to strip back interpretation.	Support for subjective and engaged interpretation of data requires that we make our histories and interpretations visible and explicit in research accounts.
Recognising who is privileged in the field (and who is excluded or diminished) and how this relates to the norms of our own cultural traditions.	Extensive demographic details of research participants are provided and compared to population norms.	Extensive demographic details of research participants are provided and absences and differences in share or scope of voice, compared to our own position, are noted.
Recognising how our research practice and writing may sustain traditional positions and ideologies.	Writing strives to be 'neutral' even if this leads to conclusions which we find are uncomfortable to report 'objectively'.	Writing takes a clear, judgemental position in relation to the conclusions developed in our research accounts.

Overall, the process of employing past-oriented reflexivity in field research involves the three processes outlined at the start of this section and discussed above. In light of the discussion, addressing how these three processes take place in field research and in later, related interpretive analysis and writing leads to a revised restatement of the three past-oriented reflexivity themes, which constitute a description of what is involved in reflexive research that looks back at its *own* foundations:

(i)   Recognising that our own ideological formation shapes our initial inter-
        pretations in the field (including the fact that a critical position is *itself*
        ideological);
(ii)   Recognising who is privileged (and who is excluded or diminished) in
        the field and how this relates to the norms of our own cultural traditions;
        and
(iii)   Recognising how our research practice and writing may sustain tradi-
        tional positions and ideologies.

As with future-oriented reflexivity, the implementation of past-oriented reflexivity differs if the research aim is either generalisability, or authenticity and resonance. The processes and outcomes, in each case, are summarised in Table 2.2.

The main differences here lie in our presence and visibility in both the research context and in the account of the study, as well as what that means for our responsibility in relation to both. If I am fully present and engaged in the research in an authentic way (or at least, doing my best to live up to that objective) it is difficult and perhaps inappropriate to take a neutral position in relation to the insights that arise. In addition, I think a neutral position is hard to square with our embodied, emotional and relational connections in the field – a point I will expand on at length in the next chapter.

2.5   RESEARCH REFLEXIVITY: A SELF-REINFORCING PROCESS

In the preceding sections future-oriented reflexivity and past-oriented reflexivity have largely been treated separately, in order to offer a clear characterisation of each. However, each temporal orientation can have a role in the development of the other kind and form a cycle, as shown in Figure 2.1.

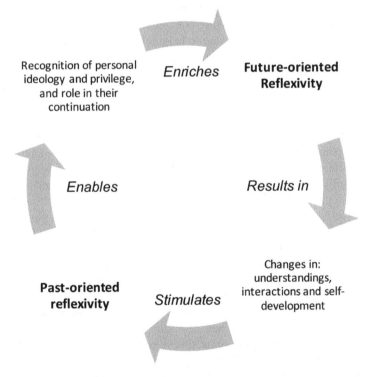

Figure 2.1   The research reflexivity cycle

Past-oriented reflexivity has an important place in helping researchers remove constraints on future-oriented reflexivity, through enriching our perspective. That is, past-oriented reflexivity helps to explain why we tend to resist taking new understandings on board: because they disturb previously unchallenged and taken-for-granted ideas that we have found easy to inhabit. Opening up our traditions and our own socio-historic construction, through past-oriented reflexivity, is therefore both helpful and uncomfortable. It is helpful because it allows us to have more insight about how we arrive at our research inter-pretations, through the ideologies and our situation in relation to patterns of privilege that hand us certain lenses. It is uncomfortable because it shows us our role in the continuation of those ideologies and patterns of privilege, if we leave them unchallenged. As summarised in Table 2.2, that discomfort is magnified by the choice between: attempts to write ourselves out of research accounts, which favours generalisability and feels safe, but lacks the resonance to engage others who are involved in the situations we research; and writing ourselves into research accounts, which will be more authentic and impactful for those with an interest in the situation, but may leave us feeling vulnerable and exposed. While we can choose to maximise either the generalisability or the authenticity and resonance of our insights, there are personal consequences as well as research outcomes that need to be considered in each case.

By examining the socialised constraints that influence our patterns of interpretation (Bourdieu, 2004; Nicholls, 2009; Parker, Racz & Palmer, 2020), we can tell our research stories differently. We may try to maximise the critical distance from our narratives (Raelin, 2008; Reynolds, 1998) or alter-natively place ourselves squarely within them (Hibbert, Sillince, Diefenbach & Cunliffe, 2014; Namatende-Sakwa, 2018; Sklaveniti & Steyaert, 2020). Importantly, *either* choice overcomes the resistance to changing and adapting, by allowing us to understand ourselves differently. In that way either choice also potentiates more thoughtful engagement in future-oriented reflexivity, in the generality of our lives and in the specifics of research practice. This leads to an important point; being a reflexive researcher requires an examination of your own patterns of interpretation and action, and if that is taken seriously it has consequences beyond the limits of any specific research project.

A genuine examination of the influences of our own past must have the effect that we will be changed through research experiences, rather than just conducting a study with detached neutrality (Hibbert, Beech, Callagher & Siedlok, 2021). The new position is always enriching, since new understand-ings constitute new perspectives on previously unexamined traditions, but they do not erase our knowledge of them, nor completely remove our reliance on them (Brown, 2004; Hibbert & Huxham, 2010; Shils, 1981). We can look through *both* the old and the new lenses and in that way future-oriented reflexivity will be better able to challenge our understandings, interactions and the self-development trajectory (as summarised in Table 2.1) that, in turn, stimulates past-oriented reflexivity. In this way, we can enter into a pattern of deliberate self-change, if we take reflexivity seriously; this pattern becomes intrinsic to a scholarly approach to life. Overall, the future and past orientations of reflexivity each have a role in the enhancement of the other, in a self-reinforcing cycle that ties personal learning and change into research processes.

2.6   CONCLUSION

This chapter has established the connections between everyday reflexivity – as a normal and inalienable aspect of human life – and reflexivity as a deliberately applied process in (interpretive) research. It has established two processes that are connected in a cyclical way, namely: (i) future-oriented reflexivity, which describes how we adapt in response to our interpretation of experiences in our social context, in order to go on with everyday life; and (ii) past-oriented reflexivity, which describes how we direct our critical thinking towards the foundations on which we build our understanding, in order to question whether there are other ways of interpreting experience that can lead us to approach the next instance of future-oriented reflexivity differently. On the one hand, these processes can be applied with a view to producing accounts of research that favour generalisability, in order to connect with others on the basis of trans-ferable claims that fit multiple contexts. On the other hand, these processes can be used to support the construction of accounts that favour authenticity, accounts which still connect with others through narratives that resonate with their situations rather than theorising about them. There is a need to consider how both of these approaches are resourced, through mobilising our awareness of ourselves as embodied, emotional, rational and relational individuals; it is through these forms of awareness that the interpretations of experience that support reflexive practice are captured. I turn to those forms of awareness, as well as the reflexive practices associated with them, in the next chapter.

Dialogue

1. I have argued that a commitment to reflexive research will (or should) have effects on how researchers develop in their everyday lives as well as allowing them to execute their research in a certain way. How does this idea affect you?
2. The alternative reasons for implementing reflexivity in research pro-cesses have been described as favouring generalisability or favouring

authenticity and resonance. I think it is not possible to do both well. Do you have counter arguments?

3. The interaction between past- and future-oriented reflexivity is messy and iterative, especially when we may be working with recollections which can have an effect on both. How might you manage this messiness?

3. Reflexive practice

My mother died suddenly when I was literally on the other side of the world. I managed to make the arrangements to change my flight home and get on a plane the next day, flying out of Brisbane at 2am. I was holding it together.
There was a long layover in Hong Kong before the final flight to London. I had access to a lounge which I was grateful for, because wandering around the terminal was out – I felt like hiding. But I was holding it together.
The lounge had showers, so I took the opportunity to freshen up, anything to eat up the time. I was holding it together. I stepped into the warm shower, normally a relaxing space... and felt the grief literally like a punch to my guts. I doubled over, howling and sobbing, curled on the shower floor in a foetal position. I was not holding it together.

3.1 REFLEXIVE PRACTICE AND LIVED EXPERIENCE

Opening this chapter with the story about my flight home following my mother's death was difficult. There were other times when the grief was almost unbearable, but nothing connects me to those feelings as closely as that moment, naked and alone, in an anonymous airport lounge thousands of miles from home. I cannot think about it without touching that raw grief again, even though many years have passed. However, I wanted to share the story since I thought it may be a powerful example of how we deal with significant experiences, in ways that are not always led by rational thought. This opens up space to talk about embodiment (a punch to the guts) and emotion (howling and sobbing) in reflexive practice, whether we are focussed on the future, or finding new ways to understand important events from the past.

The story also hints at the role of the relational context in how we deal with experiences too. Some of my friends, who are skilled in helping those with grief, have not been surprised about my experience of breaking down when I was completely alone after hours on a packed plane. Although I did not realise it at the time, removing myself from observers released me from relational constraints. There was something of a rational aspect in play too, since I was deliberately focussed on holding it together, trying to behave according to presumed norms of how I should behave in public. Is it possible to howl with anguish on a plane, surrounded by strangers? I don't know.

Reflecting on the small but significant story of my flight home also under-lines the importance of recognising the past- and future-oriented aspects of reflexivity in all their messy overlap. It also leads to thought about what that messiness means for reflexive practice in research as well as everyday life. Major life (and research) experiences and our stories of how we deal with them often contain numerous questions about what we should do, in order to be the person we want to be. We can find ourselves revisiting (and re-feeling) such experiences, as well as the questions they pose, long after the event.

3.2   FUTURE-ORIENTED AND PAST-ORIENTED REFLEXIVITY IN PRACTICE

One of the obvious differences between future-oriented and past-oriented reflexivity is the level of conscious choice that is *necessary* for the process to go on. Future-oriented reflexivity happens whether we are aware of it or not (Archer, 2007; Hibbert, Coupland & MacIntosh, 2010) as we inevitably adapt to our changing circumstances, even if the change is abrupt, sudden and unexpected. Past-oriented reflexivity, in contrast, requires deliberate engagement on our part. Despite this key difference between the orientations, future-oriented reflexivity can still be engaged with deliberately – but we have to catch it. Catching processes that would otherwise proceed automatically, deliberately engaging with them, and integrating them with more conscious processes is at the heart of reflexive practice.

To date, the literature has tended to focus on cognitive conceptualisations of reflexive practice (Myers, 2010). Even when embodied (Hardy & Hibbert, 2012), emotional (Hibbert, Callagher, Siedlok, Windahl & Kim, 2019) or rela-tional (Cutcher, Hardy, Riach & Thomas, 2020; Hibbert, Sillince, Diefenbach & Cunliffe, 2014) insights are added to the mix, little is said about what reflexive practice looks like on these levels and the assimilation into cognitive, rational processes is rapidly enacted. That is, the experiences on any level that can inform reflexivity are usually quickly appropriated to inform reflexive prac-tice, through providing ways of thinking, then scrutinised through approaches that pay attention to the patterns present in our thinking (Hibbert, Coupland & MacIntosh, 2010; Hibbert, 2013). However, there is more than thinking going on in the processes and practices of reflexivity. The remainder of this chapter, therefore, seeks to set out different levels of reflexive practice that include (but go beyond) rational thought and the distinctive kinds of awareness required for engagement at each level. The argument proceeds in five main parts. First, embodied reflexivity and interoception (an awareness of what is going on within our bodies; Hardy & Hibbert, 2012) are considered. Second, emotional reflexivity and perception – the awareness of our emotional state (and perhaps that of others) and how we act in response to those emotional states (Hibbert,

Callagher, Siedlok, Windahl & Kim, 2019) are discussed. Third, rational reflexivity and apperception (how we interpret experience in relation to what we already know: Hibbert, Siedlok & Beech, 2016; Hibbert, Beech & Siedlok, 2017), involving contextualisation and conceptualisation, are considered. In the fourth part, relational reflexivity (how our understandings can be enlarged, and our actions reshaped through open engagement with others: Hibbert, Sillince, Diefenbach & Cunliffe, 2014) and the linked processes of reception (of insights from another) and resolution (of incompatibilities in ideas through, for example, dialogue: Hibbert, Siedlok & Beech, 2016) are set out. The final section brings the main insights from the preceding sections together, to draw out general implications for reflexive practice.

3.3 EMBODIED REFLEXIVITY AND INTEROCEPTION

There are different ways of understanding embodiment, which can include (inter alia) naturalistic, symbolic, phenomenological, cultural and discursive approaches (Perry & Medina, 2015). Some of these experiential perspectives relate to how we are received or reacted to by others as embodied persons, and link to relational insights and are probably best considered from that point of view (to which I turn later). However, in this section the focus is very much on how we understand ourselves as embodied in a naturalistic sense and how that experience influences our future-oriented, adaptive reflexivity. This also involves a necessary connection to emotions, which will also be expanded on later.

Thus, for now, the focus is on a more-or-less internal perspective on our biological make-up, thinking about how we are aware of what is going on with(in) our bodies, and why that can matter. Nevertheless, in engaging with this theme, it is important to be aware that there will always be some interaction with other levels of awareness without over-theorising about those connections at this stage. With that in mind, a useful starting place for thinking about embodied reflexivity in a naturalistic frame is to pay attention to research that has looked at physiological processes within us, both at the level of awareness and at the level of the underlying mechanisms. Connecting with that material means engaging approaches to scientific research that differ from the normal slant of this book – but I hope to show why this is useful and helpful.

From a natural sciences perspective, awareness of what is happening to and within our bodies is *interoception* (Hardy & Hibbert, 2012; Tsakiris & De Preester, 2019). This is a complex and emergent area of biological and medical science, but Berntson, Gianaros and Tsakiris (2019, p. 3) offer the following definition:

> *Interoception is a multidimensional construct, broadly encompassing the process-*
> *ing of afferent (sensory) information arising from internal organs, tissues and cells*
> *of the body. This afference contributes [...] to the generation and regulation of*
> *cognitive and emotional behaviors.*

Afferent information (the messages we receive from our bodies) from intero-ception is normally grouped into two sources (Berntson, Gianaros & Tsakiris, 2019): *somatic* afference from the structural elements of the body (joints, muscles, skin and so on); and *visceral* afference arising from the body's internal organs and tissues (which includes sensory information related to taste and smell). Different aspects of interoceptive capability have also been characterised, namely:

> ... *interoceptive sensibility (i.e. the disposition to focus on bodily processes),*
> *interoceptive accuracy/sensitivity (i.e. the ability to detect internal bodily processes*
> *accurately), and interoceptive awareness (i.e. the metacognitive awareness of being*
> *accurate)* ... (Van den Bergh, Zacharioudakis & Petersen, 2019, p. 212)

Some interoception is obvious. For example, an awareness of your breathing, knowing if you are in pain, sensing what's happening with your digestion, and perhaps feeling your heart thumping (with more or less accuracy – Quadt, Critchley & Garfinkel, 2019), are all likely to be familiar experiences. However, some of what is happening is interpreted by the body 'automatically' and we do not have an awareness of the bodily systems that are responding. For example, our hormonal and autonomic nervous systems regulate our inter-nal organs and automatic bodily responses (such as fight-or-flight) without cognitive intervention. However, we can feel their effects, or recognise the role of these systems in processes at another level. For example, in receiving some shocking news that is likely to make us angry – let's say, finding out our employer has breached our trust (Driver, 2015) – our heart rate will drop briefly as we process the news, before elevating as we begin to process the information (Hardy & Hibbert, 2012) as our sympathetic nervous system guides the body to prepare for physical action. We will not be aware of the body's systems acting, but we may feel our hearts thumping as they do so, which can increase our stress and agitation.

Paying attention to the raised heart rate on reception of the news fits in with a sense of reflexive awareness, but that may not be helpful if we do not pay attention to the onset of the physical reaction in context and misattribute it to the wrong cause. Hardy and Hibbert (2012, pp. 16–17) explain and exemplify this issue in this way:

> *Schachter and Singer's two-factor theory of emotion suggests that individuals inter-pret their physiological states in the light of the cues available to them (Schachter & Singer, 1962). This was demonstrated by Dutton and Aron who looked at the behaviour of men who had just crossed a rather frightening 450' long cable sus-pension bridge over Capilano Canyon in Vancouver, which had a tendency to sway, tilt and wobble, potentially allowing the individual to fall over the low handrails to the rocks 230' below. These men were compared with men who had crossed a stout cedar bridge which was only 10' above a small shallow rivulet. In each case the men were interviewed by an attractive female researcher and the dependent variable was the number telephoning the lab to speak with her further for more information. 9/18 of the participants crossing the wobbly suspension bridge telephoned the lab whereas only 2/16 of those crossing the firm control bridge did so (for a male control interviewer the figures were 1/6 and 2/7 respectively) (Dutton & Aron, 1974). The authors speculated that the men were psychologically and physiologi-cally aroused by crossing the bridge and misattributed this arousal as attraction to the female researcher, hence the increased number of telephone calls. Effectively these individuals were likely to have physiological signs of arousal, such as elevated heart rate, which they interocepted. They then interpreted this as being due to the presence of the attractive researcher rather than the bridge they had just crossed. Hence their interoception altered their psychological state...*

There are many ways in which we could unpack and question Dutton and Aron's (1974) research, but with reflexive practice in mind it helps to draw out an important point about interoception. That is, our inward bodily awareness needs to be captured alongside the details of the context in the moment of awareness, if we are to understand what is going on and where it is 'coming from'. Indeed, there is a strongly suggested correlation between poor intero-ceptive accuracy (e.g., in relation to heart rate) and *alexythimia*, an impaired awareness of emotional states in oneself and others (Quadt, Critchley & Garfinkel, 2019). As an aside, that is one of the reasons that I find it useful to wear a smartwatch that monitors my heart rate; I find it useful in situations that are likely to be stressful, exciting or both, as a way of checking in with how my bodily reactions are developing.

The link to emotions is an important aspect of the regulative function of interoception. Berntson, Gianaros and Tsakiris (2019) report on the case of an individual (MM) who received nerve surgery. The surgery was performed to disrupt the efferent function (instruction-sending to internal organs, rather than receiving messages back from them) of part of the autonomic nervous system, in order to control excessive sweating. The side effect was the simultaneous interruption of the receiving mechanism for afferent information, via interoception through this part of the nervous system. This had serious side effects, as reported by the patient:

> *It is my experience that following this surgery there is a shift in personality and how the emotions are experienced. It is, however, not only emotional blunting but also an impaired impulse control and disinhibition (as if a grown-up brain has been replaced by a primitive, and at times manic brain, that affects higher functioning). I am not sure how to describe it really... There is an indifference and striking lack of fear...* (Berntson, Gianaros & Tsakiris, 2019, p. 8)

In contrast, better interoceptive function, especially in relation to visceral sensations, has been connected with more effective emotion regulation and richer emotional experiences (Critchley & Harrison, 2013). Moreover, it often becomes evident to an individual when there is a lack of interoceptive accuracy. For example, while I was writing this book, I had a health scare, which gave me a reason to be anxious about my heart rate. After coming home from a number of hospital tests I was sitting on the couch and looked at my smart-watch, which (as mentioned earlier) is able to measure my heart rate. Normally in that state of relaxation my heart rate would be around 60 or less, and it was 110! Then 125! I reach for my phone to call an ambulance... But of course, you will have noticed the important contextual details are not related to posture or a presumed state of relaxation, but instead are the fact that I'd had a "health scare", was "anxious" and had just had a "a number of hospital tests". The "health scare" could have indicated an alarming condition but turned out to be pretty much just a scare and nothing more. The hospital tests eventually eliminated the most alarming possibilities and confirmed a trivial problem.

Much like the men crossing the cable suspension bridge in Dutton and Aron's (1974) study, my experiences had left me in an aroused state (in this case, through anxiety) that could lead to inappropriate action. Moreover, interoception has a role in our experience of time; the effects of emotional experiences on the apparent dilation or contraction of time are enhanced by paying attention to our bodily reactions (Wittman & Meissner, 2019). The impact on our experience of time means that periods of serious stress or pain feel much longer than calm, pain-free periods. This provides more of a focus on the pain or stress, along with the stimulation of emotions. My health scare experience, feeling that my body was 'going wrong' was associated with misperceptions about the nature and significance of interoceptive information and heightened emotions over a relatively short time that 'felt longer'.

In contrast to situations when we 'read the signals wrong', better emotional awareness and regulation through better interoceptive accuracy helps us to feel more 'at home' in our bodies (Gallagher, 2000) with a more stable sense of self (Babo-Rebelo & Tallon-Baudry, 2019). Thus, Allen and Tsakiris (2019) connect the dynamic interaction and balance between interoception and exteroception (sensory experience of the world about us) with maintenance of the stability of our sense of self in a given context. Knowing what is going on with our bodies lets us feel more settled in our sense of self. Being more aware of our bodily selves in this way has also been shown to help us be more aware of others (Berntson, Gianaros & Tsakiris, 2019; Fotopolou & Tsakiris, 2017).

Despite the emerging importance of visceral sensations, as reported in recent literature, Leder (2019) argues that interoception and awareness of bodily states are often regarded as inferior interior information in contrast to rational thoughts. For that reason, we are not trained to develop our interoceptive sensitivities. However, given the link to our emotions and their regulation (Berntson, Gianaros & Tsakiris, 2019; Critchley & Harrison, 2013), our sense of time (Wittman & Meissner, 2019) and awareness of self and others (Berntson, Gianaros & Tsakiris, 2019; Fotopolou & Tsakiris, 2017; Quadt, Critchley & Garfinkel, 2019), reflexive practice cannot ignore our embodiment and the sensations that go along with that. Both everyday life and our research projects can benefit from the development of an interoceptive sensibility that pays attention to the accuracy and sensitivity of our sensations in forms of practice that support such awareness (Van den Bergh, Zacharioudakis & Petersen, 2019).

In summary, interaction with the environment, including, of course, in our research studies, occurs directly through our bodies and how our bodies respond is relevant. In addition, we enter the field with our bodies always already in an active state, and our internal processes can have effects on emotional experiences and influence our cognition, both of which impact our interpretation of events. Thus, reflexive research benefits from the cultivation of awareness of our bodily sensations, namely *interoception*, and consideration of the effects that these sensations are having.

3.4 EMOTIONAL REFLEXIVITY AND PERCEPTION

The consideration of embodiment and reflexivity, set out above, has already established connections to emotion. But recent research has also begun to direct substantial attention towards emotion and reflexivity as an important theme in its own right. A number of authors have suggested that it is in fact an essential focus and their arguments support a view that reflexivity *intrinsically* involves emotion (Brown & de Graaf, 2013; Burkitt, 2012; Holmes, 2010). Burkitt's (2012, p. 469) position in relation to the unavoidable importance of emotion for reflexivity is particularly persuasive:

> In reflexive dialogue, feelings and emotions are not just attendants to reflexivity; they are the basis and motive for reflexive thought. Reflexivity does not emerge from out of nowhere, nor is its source the various founts of knowledge: behind every

> *thought is the emotional-volitional sphere and this is true also of reflexive thought. Furthermore, our thoughts are always coloured by emotion so that we never see the world in a neutral way. Our knowledge is formed and shaped by our feelings about the world and the others with whom we interact and, thus, by our emotional relations to it and to them.*

However, advocates for the role of emotions in reflexivity have noted that their position is not the dominant approach in the field. Instead, they suggest that the majority view has a tendency to down-play emotion in accounts of research. As Gilmore and Kenny (2015, p. 71) put it:

> *...existing approaches to researcher self-reflexivity are lacking owing to their tendency to downplay the emotional experience of the ethnographer. In the method we used, however, emotion emerged as key. We saw how the research experience – and discussion of the research experience – was infused with anxiety, a strong sense of attachment, warmth and belonging to the organisation along with a related aversion to discussing this in later writing, and feelings of guilt upon departure.*

Gilmore and Kenny (2015) focus on ethnographic work, but arguably their insights also apply to other forms of interpretive research where emotions have typically and similarly been suppressed in formal accounts. The suppression of emotion in this way interferes with reflexive practice and the possibilities for learning and change within and from the research study (Burkitt, 2012). Against that, Mills and Kleinman (1988) argue that some forms of human action may *not* involve either emotion or reflexivity. An absence – or low level of engagement with – emotion can be associated with routine, habitual actions or circumstances in which individuals have cultivated rational engagement, for example the idea of professional distance amongst some clinicians. I think it can be argued, however, that the emotional response in the latter case is not absent, but it is simply another powerful example of suppression; in that case the suppression of emotion occurs in the midst of practice itself, as well as in descriptions of it. Even if Mills and Kleinman (1988) are correct in their view that emotions and reflexivity may be absent in some routine areas of action, the focus of research studies can often include matters of the opposite kind that are intrinsically emotional, for example situations that touch on the impact of suffering or death (Evans, Ribbens McCarthy, Bowlby, Wouangoa & Kébé, 2017; Laing & Moules, 2014; Lehmann, Hansen & Hurme, 2020; Miller, 2002). Overall, most areas of human behaviour worthy of study in social and organisational contexts necessarily involve emotion on some level (Lindebaum, 2017).

When emotions *are* actively considered, it is important to acknowledge that they represent a complex area of study and that particular emotional experiences can be difficult to describe and delimit. Emotions may be simple and close to embodied reactions (for example, fear or anger) or complex constructs (for example, compassion) that are closer to rational engagement because they involve specific interpretations of a particular situation. In general, it is difficult to set the boundaries purely on one level. Indeed, there is evidence that emotions are often blurred with physiological processes at one level of analysis and with cognitive processes at another level (Immordino-Yang, 2016).

A powerful example of the entanglement of emotion in reflexive practice on many levels is offered by Brown and de Graaf (2013). They showed how thinking and feeling were mutually implicated for their research participants, who were terminal cancer patients trying to craft some meaning in (and from) the time remaining to them:

> *Managing future-time, through bracketing off bad-quality time and death, and/or living with more hopeful expectations, regularly involved tensions and paradoxes [...] Hope, as already noted, is an important concept within such an analysis of tensions in thinking and feeling. As well as involving envisaged futures alongside uncertainty and possible disappointment, hope is perhaps most usefully conceptualised as an emotion.* (Brown & de Graaf, 2013, p. 557)

It has become usual, for those who acknowledge their importance, to associate emotions with *self*-reflexivity (and thus a future orientation) as in Brown and de Graaf's (2013) study. However, emotions can also have a role in other aspects of reflexive practice. Gray (2008, p. 947) argues that "...emotionally mediated apprehensions of the object of study and the practice of critical reflexivity cannot be separated when conducting research". She makes the case that emotions are central to how we perceive the focus of a study, how we attach to those within the study context and the degree to which we care about the knowledge we are seeking to produce. That argument is concordant with Immordino-Yang's (2016) position on the same themes. Particular emotions can lead to (or at least influence) our perspective on the situations that we study and how we are personally invested in such studies. Thus, Gray (2008) emphasises that emotional engagement should be seen to be imperative in the production of knowledge that supports change – that is, emotional insights need to be incorporated in any study that seeks to make a difference.

One way in which we make a difference is through our talk, and this helps us to drill down from general appreciation of the role of emotions to the detail of reflexive practice. Emotions are at work in reflexive practice in talk, enabling different alignments or presentations of the self to the tasks that one faces. For example, Sela-Sheffy and Leshem (2016, p. 448) describe how emotional talk is linked to the production of a dignified self, through an example in which a speaker shows an ability to:

> *[maneuver] between two self-in-interaction models – aggressiveness and detachment – [...] using or avoiding emotion talk in accordance with his different encounters' tasks, eventually producing a coherent, morally justified image of himself throughout the sequence of events...*

They argue that an awareness of the entanglement of emotions and identity work, in research settings, is therefore important in avoiding over-simplistic, face-value interpretations. Building on this and other studies, Hibbert, Callagher, Siedlok, Windahl and Kim (2019, p. 189) explain how the emotional aspect of reflexivity can be more directly connected to varieties of reflexive practice:

> *Lines of inquiry in this area have opened up in three particular directions: attention to one's own emotions in reflexive practice(s); emotions as key triggers or pivot points of change; and the ways in which negative or positive emotions impact differently on reflexive practices and individuals' willingness to take positive action in difficult circumstances.*

From their perspective, reflexive practice begins with attention to emotions, from the standpoint that emotions can signal when one's current ways of engaging and/or understanding in the context are inadequate. The lack of an immediate or easy move to rational understanding that is noticed in the emotional sensation triggers reflexive practice, in particular heightened self-reflexivity (Corlett, 2013), and opens up possibilities for adaptation even if that is difficult.

The evocation of emotions is also involved in the process of recall of personally significant experiences (Corlett, 2013), as I suggested at the outset of this chapter. However, it has also been argued that developing emotional distance from a triggering context is necessary in order to develop a new understanding of the situation that is to be reconsidered (Mcleod, 2003; Hibbert, Beech, Callagher & Siedlok, 2021). That also overlaps with the analytical remarks following the opening story in this chapter, and I think that both Corlett (2013) and Mcleod (2003) are right. Overall, learning is potentiated when ideas are connected to intrinsically meaningful, subjective emotional experiences (Immordino-Yang, 2016) that we are able to engage with through layers of reflexive practice. For this reason, Evans, Ribbens McCarthy, Bowlby, Wouangoa and Kébé (2017, p. 595) argue that by:

> *...continuing to work with our emotions and regarding our multiple, differently positioned, professional, research-based, emotional and personal selves as*

resources, we endeavour to attend to ethical aspects of researching sensitive topics, to produce 'emotionally-sensed knowledge'...

Their work emphasises that there is emotion work (Hibbert, Beech, Callagher & Siedlok, 2021) inherent in researching sensitive topics, especially when emotional reactions and understandings resonate with our own life contexts. Furthermore, reflexivity inevitably involves self-evaluation – often against the norms that we have absorbed from our social context – and that process can provoke difficult emotions, which in turn lead to resistance to the process (Garrety, Badham, Morrigan, Rifkin & Zanko, 2003). Thus Hibbert, Beech, Callagher and Siedlok (2021, p. 4) note that:

Despite the potential of the approach, pathways to reflexive learning from emotional experiences are not necessarily straightforward. Emotional reactions to challenging events can result in immediate, un-reflexive surface learning solely focused on recognising and avoiding similar situations [...] Such defensive reactions are understandable; but such emotional 'containing' can obstruct the deeper learning through self-reflexive practice that could allow us to be more 'at home in ourselves' and respond more effectively in future challenging situations...

In contrast, positive emotions, even in negative situations, seem to be strongly involved in reflexive practice (as noted in the example of Brown & de Graaf's (2013) study, described earlier). For example, Shin (2014) argues that positive emotions are linked to creativity in team settings, and that creativity is further enhanced by team reflexivity. More generally, whether negative or positive, emotions are entangled with our intuitive strategies about if, when and how to learn, as well as when and where our acquired knowledge should be applied (Immordino-Yang, 2016). Adding to the entanglement in our own strategies for interpretation and learning, we are also involved with the emotional presentations of others both in the moment and over time. Burkitt (2012, p. 471) remarks that:

Our own 'self-feeling' is coloured by the emotional stance that others take, and have taken, towards us, especially at key or formative periods of our lives, and something of this stays with us in our reflection on the social world and self. This is bound to influence the way people interpret the situation, monitor their own actions and make choices in social contexts.

In addition, social emotions, such as admiration in response to another person's virtue, can motivate us; working through physiological and cognitive pathways, such motivation heightens awareness and influences action (Immordino-Yang, 2016).

Overall, there is a strong case for including attention to emotional reflexivity as an aspect of reflexive practice, noting its connection with rational and relational aspects. As Holmes (2010, p. 148) comments:

> *Reflexivity is not simply a rational calculation of the amount of satisfaction an aspect or way of life brings, but is infused with feelings about how it fits (or does not) with others and what they think, feel and do. Reflexivity is emotional and comparative and relies on interpreting emotions.*

In terms of reflexive practice, the goal of recognising the potential of emotional insights and engagement with emotional reflexivity is therefore to enhance our *perception.* Experience of interaction with our environment, including relationships with other people is usually accompanied by an emotional response that precedes rational engagement; it is possible to raise our awareness of our *perception* of these feelings and their impact on how we think more-or-less rationally and make connections with others.

3.5   RATIONAL REFLEXIVITY: APPERCEPTION, CONTEXTUALISATION, CONCEPTUALISATION

Rational reflexivity is often what people have in mind when they mention reflexivity (Myers, 2010). Rational reflexivity can be conceptualised as a process of thinking about our thinking; it entails a shift from using cognitive tools, to deciding whether we have the right tools or should be using such tools at all (Hibbert, Coupland & MacIntosh, 2010). It also entails the idea that reflexivity is a process that we can apply thoughtfully and selectively in the processes of interpretive research (Alvesson, Hardy & Harley, 2008; Weick, 1999). Rational reflexivity, seen this way, is a matter of choice. We decide to employ it, avoid it, or adopt it up to a certain point of convenience. For example, Alvesson, Hardy and Harley (2008) locate choices about reflexivity in how researchers work with their materials. Their approach deploys alternate foci, shifting between deconstructing and reconstructing meaning in and from research material and experiences. Rationally reflexive choices are enacted in and through the construction of texts in this way, in the processes of research.

In a similar way, Ripamonti, Galuppo, Gorli, Scaratti and Cunliffe (2017) construct a form of rational reflexive practice that involves a 'writing grid', albeit to help individuals notice emotional reactions that are connected to situations they regard as significant, in order to move on to describing the context and how the situation was conceptualised by the individual. However, they also add a relational element to their process by working with research participants in group dialogue processes, which are used to open up alternative interpretations and explanations of the situation. For practitioners in the research context, this serves to build up an understanding of 'how things work' in the focal context and allows future learning to be built on that. It also brings researchers' own practices and ways of working into view as they seek to build connections between theory and practice.

The two approaches discussed above have key differences as well as commonalities. Alvesson, Hardy and Harley's (2008) approach to developing theory and practice connections is pragmatic and instrumental, taking on board reflexive practice enough to be able to speak from and about a research study. At the same time their approach avoids being silenced by the concerns of radical reflexivity (Cunliffe, 2003) or engagement with a more complex struggle to integrate insights from complex, multi-party dialogue when relational aspects begin to have an influence, as in the alternate approach offered by Ripamonti, Galuppo, Gorli, Scaratti and Cunliffe (2017). Both are nevertheless hybrid positions; they accept that for rational reflexive practice to engage with the past in a way that enables us to go on speaking, it cannot be taken to its ultimate limit. This is sensible, but it is also a good argument for other levels of reflexive practice to be brought alongside rationality in the process, to avoid researchers being drawn too easily towards convenient explanations – thus Ripamonti, Galuppo, Gorli, Scaratti and Cunliffe's (2017) method, with its clear connections to other levels, does offset that to a degree.

While the possible choices about how to apply rational reflexive practice in research studies mean that it can be operationalised in deliberate ways, as the examples above show, there is still a need for reflexive practice is more general and addresses deeper concerns. Sklaveniti and Steyaert (2020, p. 313) argue that:

> ...reflexivity is not so much a self-involved scholarly issue but rather a matter of attending to the social and intellectual unconscious embedded in our research and analytical tools...

As such, they align with a view of rational reflexive practice as a way of opening up, to critical examination, both what lies in our formative contexts and how we conceptualise what is there. Similarly, McLean, Harvey and Chia (2012) explored how accumulated experience informs rational reflexive practice, through recognising useful knowledge and developing experience-informed strategies for future action. Interestingly, the empirical material they collected also showed how their research participants, senior executives looking back on elite business careers, constructed rationally reflexive narratives that shifted from past difficulties to optimistic outlooks and opportunism. This shifting pattern in their narratives shows how past-oriented reflexive practice can be woven into future-oriented practice through connections at an emotional level. Building on their insights, it is possible to see oneself as embedded in and constructed by a formative process (Hibbert, Beech & Siedlok, 2017). Allowing for these formational effects in theoretical accounts of our research can help our ideas be closer, and more faithful, to practice.

There is, however, a problem associated with emphasising choice in rational reflexivity in any of the preceding approaches. The difficulty is that there is no neutral place to stand where we can make an 'objective' evaluation of the contexts that formed our perspectives and led us to question them (Cunliffe, 2003; Hibbert, Coupland & MacIntosh, 2010). For this reason, rational reflexivity does not lead to the elimination of individual perspectives and ways of thinking, even if it is engaged with quite deliberately; instead, it guides us towards the contexts that our ways of thinking 'come from'. This means that when we develop everyday or formal theories based on our experiences (including research experiences), rational reflexive practice helps us to understand the limitations that are intrinsic to those theories (Hibbert, Sillince, Diefenbach & Cunliffe, 2014; Ripamonti, Galuppo, Gorli, Scaratti & Cunliffe, 2017; Sklaveniti & Steyaert, 2020).

Collien (2018) adds to such debates on the constrained and situated nature of rational reflexivity by drawing our attention to inequalities and differences in the research context. She highlights the need for critical attention to the distribution of power (including a given researcher's status in the field), the researcher's embeddedness within social categories (such as class or gender) and the effects of the scholarly point of view, which emphasise distanciation and increase the disconnection of interpretations from practice. All of these are potentially significant influences on how we have arrived at our choices and interpretations in the field. Trying to unravel these influences can be problematic, especially when the goal is to break down barriers with practice and practitioners. For example, Iszatt-White, Kempster and Carroll (2017) argue that an explicit focus on differences and power imbalances, in an attempt to challenge or deconstruct them, can have the effect of simply reinforcing them through increased attention. That is, the effect of this extra attention is to make the differences and imbalances seem *more*, rather than *less* real. They suggest addressing this paradox through a rhythm of reflexive interludes and interruptions which are interleaved with traditional practice (cf. Hibbert & Huxham, 2010) and developing a focus of joint interest to reshape 'power over' individuals into the more productive form of collective 'power to' achieve outcomes collaboratively (Huxham & Vangen, 2005).

Following Iszatt-White, Kempster and Carroll's (2017) advice can be difficult since sometimes we may be more or less aware, and more or less honest, about our situated perspective and experience. For example, McDonald (2016), through his exploration of queer reflexivity in the field, expands the idea of 'the closet' to a general metaphor for a crucial aspect of field research, in order to address this problem. He shows how all researchers make more-or-less rational choices about the extent to which they disclose or perform aspects of themselves in their research contexts. However, this aspect of rational reflexive practice has blurred edges, since our disclosures are affected relationally by our receptiveness to normative expectations in the context on one level, as well as being affected emotionally on another level by the climate of inclusion or exclusion that such expectations create.

Thus, there is good support for Winterburn's (2020) argument that there is a need to avoid becoming too settled and comfortable in our research contexts. She highlights how discomforting moments can provide opportunities to challenge the completeness or universality of our rational conceptualisations. Her work also connects to relational perspectives, since the moment of uneasiness that she uses as an example comes from the resistance of another to the progress of a learning process. The process was assumed to be neutral, however it was not experienced in that way. Similarly, from his experience of the Quakers' consensual process for organisation, Allen (2017) offers insights for rational reflexive practice by introducing the need to develop the capacity for unknowing. His account of the process involves listening to the meaningfulness of silences, extending the horizon for reaching consensus through thoughtful questions, and expecting consensus to be reached in dialogue that includes both silence and talk. This is, of course, also relevant to our understanding of relational reflexive practice.

Overall, engaging with rational reflexivity involves two kinds of focal awareness, namely contextualisation and conceptualisation. Each event is contextualised, by giving an account of the situatedness of the individual's experience. That is, contextualisation describes how we turn our awareness on ourselves, to look into our past leading up to a situated moment of experience, to see what we bring to an event of interpretation (Collien, 2018; Cunliffe, 2003; Gadamer, 1998; Hibbert, Coupland & MacIntosh, 2010; McLean, Harvey & Chia 2012; Sklaveniti & Steyaert, 2020). It is then conceptualised in order to render the interpretation of experience in a comprehensible way to support the development of possible implications for ongoing thought and practice. Conceptualisation therefore describes how we talk, narrate or write about that moment of experience in order to render visible the meaning we draw from it (Alvesson, Hardy & Harley, 2008; Hibbert, Sillince, Diefenbach & Cunliffe, 2014; Ripamonti, Galuppo, Gorli, Scaratti & Cunliffe, 2017). Taking these two aspects together, rational reflexivity fundamentally involves *apperception*: the process through which experience is raised to awareness and made sense of, through rational comparative thought in relation to what is already known to us.

3.6   RELATIONAL REFLEXIVITY, RECEPTION AND RESOLUTION

Relational reflexivity is complex since, as noted in the preceding sections, there are many overlaps with embodied, emotional and rational aspects of reflexive practice. Recognising this complexity, Bissett and Saunders (2015) see relational reflexive practice as a threshold conception (Wright & Hibbert, 2015), that once adopted can enable transformational learning, particularly in connection with ethical dilemmas and challenges (cf. Hibbert & Cunliffe, 2015). But the threshold needs to be crossed in some way for the potential to be realised, which involves establishing the necessary conditions for critical conversation so that others' insights can add broaden and challenge the limits of our understanding (Larsson & Knudsen, 2021).

Rhodes and Carlsen (2018) clearly articulate the importance of being able to receive ideas from others in relational reflexive practice; that is, of being influenced by the insights of others however they are formed and communicated (Hibbert, Sillince, Diefenbach & Cunliffe, 2014). In other words, the underpinning of their position is that:

> *To approach the other ethically means to accept their alterity as being mysterious and unrepresentable, whilst also accepting that the only tool we have to know them is representational language.* (Rhodes & Carlsen, 2018, p. 1304)

What is received in relationally reflexive encounters is not, therefore, something that is necessarily clear or easy to define. Further attention is necessary to bring about resolution, to make the possible interpretation(s) clear within a horizon of shared understanding. For example, Chilvers and Kearnes (2020, p. 348), in their work on participatory programs in civil society, advocate forms of relational reflexive practice "...that attend to their framings, emergence, uncertainties, and effects". Their approach builds on understandings of how circumstances and situations come to be interpreted as they are in the midst of their adaptive unfolding, alongside an acknowledgement of the uncertainties that participants carry into the given context.

In part, the interpretive struggle depends on the media of interaction and how they support different kinds of engagement and focus. Simon (2013, p. 14) characterises relational reflexive practice as a way of connecting multiple forms of dialogue with texts and persons, with the aim of speaking:

> *...about and from within relationships—whether, for example, from within the different voices of the researcher's inner dialogue, between the researcher(s) and other texts, between the researcher and others in outer dialogue, between writers and readers of research writing in relational contexts.*

Working in and with other media, besides writing, may also be involved in establishing the required relational connections. Ajjawi, Hilder, Noble, Teodorczuk and Billett (2020) describe how using video can facilitate the collaborative and creative development in everyday practices, through relational reflexivity.

Relational reflexive practice is not just about anodyne theoretical connection, however, since it involves embodied and emotional layers of experience too. For example, Adjepong (2019, pp. 42–43) articulated how her relational reflexivity included juxtapositions of difference and bodily encounters:

> *Within my research context, my legibility as a queer black person marked my body as matter out of place. [...] By staying, my presence likely violated the sensibilities of some of the people with whom I came into contact. Despite the discomforts and emotional distress that my embodiment sometimes generated while I was in the community [...] makes possible a profound reading of this community's organisational logics. [...] Importantly, this ethnographic performance is not about the researcher, but instead puts the researcher's history and body in conversation with the research participants' and thereby opens up possibilities for connections that may not have previously been imagined.*

Nicholls (2009) and Keevers and Treleaven (2011) also both describe relational reflexivity in terms that involve a complex interweaving of types and levels of practice. Similarly, the relational perspective adopted by Rhodes and Carlsen (2018, p. 1295) includes a focus on bodily and emotional levels of connection, along with aesthetic sensibilities:

> *...a reflexively ethical position from which to conduct research [...in which the...] promise for research is a deepening of our corporeal, affective and aesthetic engagement with others and an enlarged sense of the ethical meaning of research.*

However, relational reflexive practice need not simply be focussed, as it often is, on the micro-level of interaction (Keevers & Treleaven, 2011) and how this informs emerging practice. Instead, it may be examined longitudinally, based on the recognition of deep formational roots in the past. Lupu, Spence and Empson (2018) add this kind of interesting, deep temporal dimension to relational reflexive practice by describing how formative relationships (their focus is on families, in particular) shape ongoing interpretations and actions. They show:

> *...how dispositions embodied during one's upbringing can largely transcend time and space. These dispositions hold a powerful sway over individuals and may continue to structure action even when professionals exhibit a desire to act differently. In turn, this implies that the impediments to greater equality lie not only in organisational and societal structures, but within individuals themselves in the form of*

dispositions and categories of perception that contribute towards the maintenance
and reproduction of those structures. (Lupu, Spence & Empson, 2018, pp. 155–156)

Lupu, Spence and Empson (2018) also capture the possibility that these temporally extended effects can be disrupted through deliberate distancing, or through confronting circumstances that mandate different interpretations and choices (Meliou & Edwards, 2018). Thus, it is interesting to consider the implications of their insights more broadly, to consider who we are 'carrying with us' in shorter or longer pauses away from the immediate context of inter-personal interaction. For example, a friend and colleague, "Jane", during our shared, collaborative, autoethnographic research project, noted how relation-ships and the reflexive possibilities they bring were important in establishing how an important situation played out:

> *Relationships were a central feature of the situation; however, it wasn't until others [in this authorial team] pointed this out to me that I realised how central they were. The situation arose because of an unhealthy relationship with a colleague; my initial blocking behavior was an attempt to resist other colleagues' behavior with whom I also had relationships with. And, then it was another relationship with my then Department Head that prompted me to start looking for options to fix the situation. Initially, I looked into leaving the academy but this really wasn't what I wanted because I like what I do – it might have been different if I had found some-thing outside of the academy that I really wanted to pursue, but I didn't. I did look at PhD programs at different universities here and overseas. I was interviewed and did get offers but it still felt like running away [from the difficult situation]. I've often believed that the relationships I have with a few close colleagues are what make the difference in the [teaching and research] work we do, but by seeing reinforcing relationships as a practice, I can see that those relationships provided a way for me to move out of a difficult space without leaving the organisation ... I kind of feel like I worked through it [the difficult situation] rather than running away from it.*
> (Hibbert, Callagher, Siedlok, Windahl & Kim, 2019, p. 198)

The importance of relational reflexivity for Jane, in the extract cited above, is clear. But it is also clear that there were multiple competing relationships affecting how reflexive practice was experienced. There were multiple lines of reception (positive and negative) but the resolution of the impact of her cumulative experiences depended on Jane seeing herself as both placing trust in particular relationships and constituting her practice in the context of them. Any rendering of experience in this way introduces an implicit rational focus too; it is impossible to describe a situation and course of action without conceptualising and contextualising to some degree. However, the key here is to notice the existence and quality of particular trusting relationships. These relationships allowed for acceptance in relation to a disruptive message and confidence in taking action based on that, towards modifying one's under-standing and potentiating self-change.

Thus, in sum, relational reflexive practice involves an awareness of what we receive as valid or useful, from engagement with others in a particular relational setting, and in the context of already emerging adaptive practice. But it also involves attention to how issues and tensions between multiple interpretive possibilities in the relational setting are resolved within a shared horizon of understanding.

3.7 CONNECTIONS BETWEEN THE LEVELS

Theoretical Connections

The resolution of uncertain or conflicting insights and influences, received through particular situations of relational reflexivity, may involve other relational interactions or engagement with reflexivity on a different level. This is possible because, as has been indicated at several points in earlier sections, relational reflexivity has numerous overlaps with the other levels. Indeed, all of the levels are interconnected.

At the embodied level, Dutton and Aron's (1974) bridge experiment showed a strong and unconscious link between a triggered physical state and interpretations of interpersonal connections, with the implication that better interoception (say, attention to heart rate or breathing) might have cast the interactions in a different light. More generally, being more aware of our bodily selves has been shown to help us be more aware of others (Berntson, Gianaros & Tsakiris, 2019; Fotopolou & Tsakiris, 2017). In addition, poor interoceptive accuracy has been correlated with impaired awareness of emotional states in oneself and others (Quadt, Critchley & Garfinkel, 2019). Since the relational level also involves emotions, this is an important connection.

Connecting with Quadt, Critchley and Garfinkel's insights from a different, sociological direction, Holmes (2010) describes how the emotional level is involved in the comparisons we make in our relational contexts with others, in order to arrive at a conclusion about what is going on in a particular setting, and how we use those conclusions to guide our future action (Holmes, 2010). In short, we *feel* our way forward in our interactions with others, as we draw out plausible interpretations of what is going on in the context of these relationships.

Connections between the rational and relational levels are also important. For example, the group dialogue processes described by Ripamonti, Galuppo, Gorli, Scaratti and Cunliffe (2017) bring rational thought and critique into a space of mutual learning and change. On a broader level, Sklaveniti and Steyaert (2020) note the role of the social influences in informing our unconscious when we are engaged in rational reflexivity, aligning with the importance of the formational influence of key experiences and relationships explored by McLean, Harvey and Chia (2012). Turning our attention in the opposite direction, with an awareness of how such influences can add up to normative pressures in a given relational context (McDonald, 2016), rational critique can be applied to disrupt the reception of ideas and insights developed through relationships in particular situations.

While they are revealing (and potentially useful in shaping reflexive practice), the levels of reflexivity and the connections between them are also a potential source of philosophical debate and disagreement. This is, in part, because the ways in which these levels are conceptualised spans different paradigms. The literature on interoception (see, for example, Tsakiris & De Preester, 2019) is strongly rooted in the natural sciences and positivist approaches. Emotions (especially simple emotions like anger or fear) can be approached within the same paradigm, but complex ideas like compassion or hope might be more helpfully approached from social constructionist, inter-pretive perspectives (Hibbert, Beech, Callagher & Siedlok, 2021). Rationality is on the one hand amenable to positivist reductionism, but on the other hand – in everyday contexts – it is guided by normative rules that shape action and interpretation that might be better described from a social constructionist per-spective (McDonald, 2016). Relationality, from a positivist conceptualisation is likely to focus on *transactions between* individuals and what *each* is given or receives in the process, whereas approached from an interpretive frame it is likely to focus on *experiences or interpretations developed between* people, focussing on what occurs for them in the broad context of interaction (Hibbert, Siedlok & Beech, 2016; Hibbert, Beech & Siedlok, 2017). The interactions and tensions between these alternative perspectives adds further layers of uncer-tainty to the processes of reflexivity, when applied to our research or everyday practice. Favouring one particular perspective puts a slant on how different levels of reflexivity are applied, as well as influencing which level is preferred as the starting point for reflexive practice.

The positivist picture favours rationality, especially when an experience fits comfortably within our established frames of understanding; a conversation partner provides us with some knowledge that fits with our 'common sense' and so we acknowledge (but perhaps only internally) the need or potential to act on it. Think about a doctor telling you that you need to drink a little less, or take more exercise. Although you might not like the advice (and you may not act on it) you will be likely to acknowledge its validity.

The interpretivist picture blends emotion into the mix and sits the conver-sation or action within the context of a network of relationships. How does the advice to drink less fit with a relational context, if you live in a place like the UK with an alcohol culture, for example? How do you feel about exercise in the context of busy life involving work and family? Are there competing relationships and relationalities that immediately shift the meaning of the conversation in more complex ways? This is why the interpretivist picture can open up more interesting reflexive possibilities, because it incorporates our immediate relational situation and the pattern of other relationships, those that are past and those that are present but distant, which also have a bearing on how we understand ourselves and our experiences. In addition, an interpretive approach (or approaches, see: Cunliffe, 2011; Gill, 2014) allows paradigms *themselves* to be seen as matters of interpretation on a grand scale. For that reason, the interpretivist has the luxury of utilising the fruits of studies based on the scientific method alongside interpretive work, as long as there remains a level of critique about the framing of it and care in connection with the language used in the presentation of ideas. That is, there is a need to consider and be aware of the suppression of alternatives within a seemingly neutral scientific text (Wright, Middleton, Hibbert & Brazil, 2020).

The conclusion of this brief exploration of the connections and tensions between the different levels of reflexivity is that, from an interpretive perspective, it is necessary to bring the levels together in our reflexive practice and that we need not be overly concerned with the commensurability of the ideas we bring together in this way. Nevertheless, this integration of the levels will still be troublesome and require care; one way of approaching this challenge is articulated below.

From Levels of Reflexivity to Reflexive Practice

The links and overlaps between the different levels of reflexivity, discussed above, suggest that we cannot reduce the levels to an underlying mechanism, nor appropriate them all from within one level – as often occurs in the literature, where rational reflexivity is allowed an implicit leading role. Instead, there is a need to look at the insights that can be generated by bringing the *connections* into view. Before turning to the connections in more detail, the different levels, and the associated forms of focal awareness that are involved in reflexive practice, are first summarised in Table 3.1.

Table 3.1   *Levels of reflexivity and practices of awareness*

Level	Practice focus	Overview
Embodied	Interoception	Experience of interaction with the environment occurs directly through our bodies and how our bodies respond, and it is possible to cultivate awareness of bodily sensations, namely *interoception*, and consider their effects.
Emotional	Perception	Experience of interaction with the environment (including other people) is often accompanied by an emotional response that precedes rational engagement; it is possible to raise awareness of our *perception* of these feelings and their impact.
Rational	Apperception: Contextualisation *and* Conceptualisation	Often the main focus of reflexivity, in which experience is raised to awareness and examined through rational, critical thought in relation to what is already known (*apperception*). An experience is first of all *contextualised*, in relation to the situatedness of the individual's past experience (and a pause to examine and give an account of this situatedness is possible). It is then *conceptualised* in order to render the interpretation of experience in a way that supports the development of possible implications for ongoing thought and practice.
Relational	Reception *and* Resolution	An experience leads to insights through the communication or actions of others, that is *received* as potentially meaningful without immediate critical engagement in return; these are often words or actions that interrupt 'comfortable' thought or practice. What is received may have an impact that is unclear and be *resolved* through dialogue in particular (trusted) relationships or engagement in other layers of reflexive practice.

Attention to each of the individual levels of awareness listed in Table 3.1 can be considered as a way of constituting particular reflexive practices. However, the level of awareness that is our focus, at any given time, is not necessarily a matter of choice. We are always responding to incoming experience. How that experience is captured at a particular level may present the most immediately salient impression, but not the only possible one, in a given moment. Some examples are listed, in Table 3.2, of the kinds of impression that may bend our awareness towards a particular level.

Table 3.2   *Levels of reflexive experiences and impressions*

Level	Example experiences/impressions
Embodied	Racing heart, 'butterflies in the stomach', 'freezing', pain during an event.
Emotional	Having feelings of anger, sadness, despair, joy, grief, shame during events.
Rational	Finding forms of expression, and generating plausible ideas to explain events.
Relational	Encountering different perspectives on events and entertaining new understandings.

To engage in a deeper pattern of reflexive practice, it is helpful to deliberately shift attention from where it is immediately drawn, by looking at the other levels and how they are connected. As an example, let's say that an initial focus on interoception is prompted by some pain and discomfort from a cough. This might trigger emotions such as irritation (a cough is annoying) and sadness (who likes being ill?) Then you engage with your experience rationally, realising that you are in a context where the coronavirus is circulating and you conceptualise your illness as possible COVID-19: thereby adding fear to your mix of emotions and stimulating a new focus on interoception, as you consider whether other symptoms are present. Then you bring in the relational aspect by talking to your partner, who points out that neither of you have been in contact with anyone else for two weeks, it is peak allergy season, and what is more you are also a notorious hypochondriac. This brings new possibilities, and it is likely that these less alarming possibilities may be right. Note that a rationally reflexive response may have reached the same conclusion in due course, but bringing all the levels into play brings alternatives into view more readily.

In our reflexive practice, especially applied to research projects, there is, therefore, a need to ensure that an intense experience at one level does not lead to a lack of awareness of overlapping dynamics at other levels. Missing these connections can mislead us about what is going on. In research settings where time is often limited and our dialogue with participants may be constrained by unfamiliarity, this is a particular risk. We need to check what is behind the level of awareness that we are settled in. This is particularly the case when an assumption of rational awareness may overlook the effects of interoception and emotional perceptions, which may quickly lock us in to certain actions and interpretations (Hardy & Hibbert, 2012; Hibbert, Beech, Callagher & Siedlok, 2021). For example, I might conceptualise another person, with whom I am in conversation, as rather patronising (locating my impressions at the relational and rational level). However, by checking over emotional perceptions and interoception I realise that because of a lack of sleep I am irritable, achy and slumped in my chair. I am not presenting an impression of being alert (or even well) and my interlocutor is trying to be thoughtful and gentle by keeping things simple. This realisation gives me the chance to adjust my self-presentation (if I am able!), and/or to reconsider how I am receiving what my conversation partner is offering. Alternatively, it may enable me to bring my tiredness into the conversation, so that we can both have the chance to work around it. In research contexts, thinking about these options also helps to bring out any expectations of neutral generalisability that are at work in our assumptions about our developing insights, as opposed to a focus on authentic engagement.

In addition, of course, there are also effects in relational contexts where another's emotions or bodily presence, in relation to our own, might engender *direct* emotional effects (as discussed in relation to emotional contagion, for example: Ashkanasy, 2003; Dasborough, Ashkanasy, Tee & Tse, 2009) or trigger bodily responses in us that are noticed through interoception (Berntson, Gianaros & Tsakiris, 2019; Fotopolou & Tsakiris, 2017; Quadt, Critchley & Garfinkel, 2019). Added to which, we will of course be experiencing and characterising our emotional experience of others through the formational norms that have shaped our patterns of interpretation (Hibbert, Beech & Siedlok, 2017) and have imbued the relational context with transient structures for organising that shape practice and how it is received (Keevers & Treleaven, 2011; Lupu, Spence & Empson, 2018).

Overall, reflexive practice requires that we keep moving between different levels of awareness, to ensure that our insights are challenged from all of the embodied, emotional and rational and relational perspectives, within the reflexive cycle that moves between future- and past-orientations (see Figure 2.1, presented in Chapter 2). In this way we can have the best chance of understanding what it is that we have learned, how we arrived at that knowledge, and how we should act in response to it. This is worthwhile in the context of everyday life, but essential during engagement in interpretive research.

Dialogue

1. In this chapter one of the main themes is our awareness of our embodiment, through interoception. For some, paying attention to their bodies can be worrisome. How does this aspect of reflexive practice sit with you?
2. I have argued that we tend to integrate all of the levels of reflexive practice from within the rationally reflexive standpoint. Are there any persuasive alternatives, about which we may still speak and write?

3. The view of relational reflexive practice in this chapter largely focusses on how that practice is understood (and the insights from it captured) by an individual. From your perspective, is this truly a relational view?

4.   Reflexive practice in research processes

Early in my career, I was discussing the frustrations of trying to publish qualitative research articles with [famous professor]. I was grumbling at some length about the endless methodological questions journal reviewers raised and the tedious (and impossible) demands to let them interpret the data for themselves – as if I could give reviewers an equivalent experience to years in the field within a conventional eight-thousand-word article.

"I am also finding it impossible to describe the detailed research process I followed, in the few pages I can spare – do you have any suggestions about how I can do that?" I enquired.

He responded: "Stop trying! If we wrote up our research *exactly* how we did it, we would never get published!"

4.1   FAVOURING ACCURACY OVER PRECISION

In this chapter I explain how reflexive practices can have a role across the whole life of a research study. I set out the discussion on this topic across multiple research processes or phases, that are arranged in a linear way. As the opening vignette suggests, this arrangement is simply an organising framework and I do not suggest that all research studies have the same order or shape, or that we can describe them with precision in a concise format. In later chapters I hope to make the usual messiness of lived-out research clear by providing two quite different case studies, as examples of the many different trajectories that research projects can take as they are developed.

The organising framework I set out here involves seven research processes or phases. First, the *initial characterisation* of the research idea and *commitment to it* that we develop before any formal project is underway are discussed. Second, the process of *grounding* a potential project *in literature* to give it shape and provide a research focus is discussed. Third, the approaches to the *identification of context(s) in* which a study can be conducted are set out. Fourth, *choices about data* – how it is identified, delimited and captured – are considered. Fifth, *approaches to analysis*, which explores the how and why of developing meaning from empirical material, are explored. The sixth element involves *reconnecting to literature*, as we seek to show how our interpretations of research material can take the academic conversation in a new direction.

The final element explores the development of nascent ideas through *responding to critique*, as our work is challenged and reshaped during dissemination and publication processes.

It is important to emphasise that I am not seeking to provide a comprehensive guide to qualitative research or describe a particular method (as I have done with colleagues elsewhere: see, for example, Hibbert, Sillince, Diefenbach & Cunliffe, 2014). Instead, my aim is simply to show that reflexive practices can and should have a role in each of these processes, so you can consider how they might be useful within your *own* research approach.

4.2   CHARACTERISATION, MOTIVATIONS AND COMMITMENT

There is often an expectation that we will identify a prospect for research from our engagement with literature. There are certainly scholars who do this; those who, deeply engaged with reading in their subject area, maintain an ongoing 'conversation' with their debates in their discipline as part of long-term research interests. However, literature engagement is not the only way that projects begin, and factors other than scholarly interest are involved in moving from a possible idea to a committed project.

Taking a reflexive view, the real starting point is our *motivation*. What brings us to the point of considering scholarly research in the first place? These decisions are faced by most researchers at several key points, for example when choosing a masters dissertation topic, developing a doctoral study idea, or branching out into a new research direction at multiple points during our careers. I think it is useful to consider two possible kinds of research motivation, that I am going to label *cold* and *hot*, each of which uses reflexive practices differently.

Cold Motivation

Cold motivation begins in the typical expectation – as evidenced by the majority of academic articles across the social sciences – that a scholar has been reading the literature and has come across a gap that requires better explanation and/or new theory to fill it, or has identified a phenomenon that could be understood better from a new perspective. What follows is normally their answer to this logically derived question. Scholarly approaches of this sort have their roots in synthetic and integrative skills in working with literature, but (should) also involve: (i) rational reflexivity and the practices of contextualisation and conceptualisation, and (ii) relational reflexivity and the practices of reception and resolution.

Through the rational reflexive practice of contextualisation, we relate the potential opportunity to our situated experience (Collien, 2018; Hibbert, Coupland & MacIntosh, 2010; McLean, Harvey & Chia, 2012; Sklaveniti & Steyaert, 2020). Questions about the significance of the research idea for our developing specialisation might be in play, for example, based on earlier projects and our reading. Other issues we may entertain involve the resources necessary to engage with the opportunity, both intellectual and otherwise. Then, through conceptualisation (Alvesson, Hardy & Harley, 2008; Hibbert, Sillince, Diefenbach & Cunliffe, 2014), we structure research ideas that promise to be suitable and feasible in such a way that we have confidence to take the next step in developing a study. That is, the loose idea we have at this point is not likely to be a 'research question' that is fully formed, but instead it will be a pointer towards that, which allows us to engage in conversation to move towards a focussed line of inquiry.

From the cold motivation perspective, our intellectual interests are further sharpened through relational reflexivity. My contention is that this always happens, whether we are fully aware of it or not; however, it would be better if we paid deliberate attention to the practices in play, in two ways. First, our ideas are always shaped by our *reception* of the ideas of others that we see as authoritative (Lupu, Spence & Empson, 2018; Simon, 2013), or simply find beguiling, in ways that we cannot fully articulate (at least at first). Importantly, this is not about the rational evaluation of intellectual achievements, but rather how our formation in community has effects that play out through us. For example, it is not likely that anyone with a developed interest in hermeneutics, as an approach to research, would have a neutral opinion about the relative merits of the philosophical hermeneutics of Gadamer (1998), the critical approach of Habermas (1987a, 1987b) or deconstruction *à la* Derrida (1976, 1978). One of those authors (and their followers) is likely to be a more per-suasive foundational thinker for an interpretivist of a particular kind. We place weight on the ideas that seem to be built on foundations we trust.

Second, there may be tensions and uncertainties in our emerging ideas, which we clarify through *resolution*. That is, conversation with those with whom we have trusted relationships enables us to find a path towards possible shared understandings (Chilvers & Kearnes, 2020; Hibbert, Siedlok & Beech, 2016). The conversation with trusted colleagues is not necessarily about the intellectual rigour and robustness of a (still-emerging) research idea; it could instead be about the practicalities of going forward with a project based upon it. For example, I remember coming up with vague ideas about a focus on identity as part of my research direction for my PhD project (many years ago). Trusted senior colleagues expressed alarm about my notion of casually wandering into a theoretical domain populated by different camps at odds with each other. Identity researchers have a range of views about the ways in which the very notion of identity or identity work (Beech, Gilmore, Hibbert & Ybema, 2016; Beech, Linstead & Sims, 2007; Callagher, El Sahn, Hibbert, Korber & Siedlok, 2021) should be understood, which would make progress more demanding than I might have expected. My research went on to include identity, but in a less central way (Hibbert, MacIntosh & McInnes, 2007). This was a choice for which I was thankful, in later years.

Overall, the point of *cold motivation* is that it is guided by rational and relational reflexive practices that are focussed on practicalities and guided through community conversations. If you were wondering earlier why I styled this kind of motivation 'cold', you will probably have realised why, at this point. It is because cold motivation lacks any sense of emotional engagement or truly *personal* investment in the research idea. *Hot motivation*, discussed below, offers a defining contrast.

Hot Motivation

Hot motivation begins with something that bugs you, that you could not leave alone if you tried. These are issues that have a primary connection to personal experience on some level, perhaps through having strong associations with emotional responses and memories, or a current research issue that suddenly becomes deeply personal. A good example is provided in the work of Wright and Wright (2019) which involves a leading scholar and her daughter. The scholar, April Wright, describes how she encountered:

> …a collision between my research and personal lifeworlds. This collision occurred when I took my acutely unwell daughter to the hospital emergency department that also serves as the field site for my research. (Wright & Wright, 2019, p. 255)

These kinds of past reflections or current crises lead to an engagement in emotional reflexivity through the practice of *perception* (Evans, Ribbens McCarthy, Bowlby, Wouangoa & Kébé, 2017; Hibbert, Callagher, Siedlok, Windahl & Kim, 2019; Immordino-Yang, 2016). Such emotional dynamics can seem problematic when they emerge, as well as having effects that lead us to doubt our approach to research. However, they can make a positive difference to how we understand the situations we research that can also resonate with others. April Wright reports how:

> …a shift between researcher and mother is triggered at a health care research symposium. I have been invited to sit on a panel of experts about the future of emergency departments for an audience of emergency physicians, other clinicians, health policymakers and managers, and clinician researchers. As the only organisational researcher at the event, I am there to talk dispassionately and professionally about my insights into the future of emergency medicine based on the findings of my

extensive program of research. Yet when I am asked a question about organisational culture in emergency departments, my mother identity takes over half way through my answer. To illustrate the processes of how values and beliefs embedded within culture shape the patient experience, I recount some of my personal experiences as the mother of a patient in the emergency department. I make no reference to the extensive examples in the empirical dataset that took years of observations and interviews to collect. My researcher identity groans. Shut up, mum. When several members of the audience seek me out afterwards to say they were inspired by my personal story and ask questions about my research findings, my researcher identity is somewhat appeased. (Wright & Wright, 2019, p. 266)

This kind of hot motivation can be about life experience within the context of a critical incident or a particular study – as for Wright and Wright (2019) – or about formative experiences that shape us as researchers. I think, for example, of Nancy Moules' hermeneutic approach, developed through working with colleagues to develop approaches to cancer care, approaches that recognise the importance of interpreting the lived experience of patients and their families (for example, Laing & Moules, 2014; Laing, Moules, Sinclair & Estefan, 2020; Moules, Jardine, McCaffrey & Brown, 2013; Moules, McCaffrey, Field & Laing, 2015). She traces her motivation and the development of her approach to her experience as a nurse caring for children with terminal cancer, along with their families. She began her research career after caring for fifty-five children who died, each and every one of whom mattered to her deeply. It's hard to be dispassionate about that kind of experience (and I don't think anyone should be) and it helps me to identify another aspect of hot motivation. Alongside emotional *perception*, it may also involve embodied experience and *interoception*. Reading and thinking about Moules' work and that of her colleagues sometimes makes me cry, but I feel it in my gut and my eyes before I have perceived the emotion. Indeed, I am not sure how to label the emotion I experience… sadness? vicarious grief? empathetic sorrow? Somehow describing the physical sensations is much clearer. It makes me cry. I feel it in my gut. Responding to this kind of reflexive awareness has opened up, for me, some research ideas that are centrally concerned with emotion, how it is experienced and the implications of that (see, for example, Hibbert, Beech, Callagher & Siedlok, 2021; Hibbert, Callagher, Siedlok, Windahl & Kim, 2019; Irving, Wright & Hibbert, 2019).

Whichever way hot motivation 'gets you', emotional and embodied levels of reflexivity are important. Giving an account of how your choice and development of a research idea is linked to reflexive practices of perception and interoception will be important in introducing an authentic story of the research that follows. It will also be an important aspect of your commitment to the research area.

Commitment to Research: Blending The Hot and the Cold

Commitment to a research project is unlikely to involve just one or the other of hot or cold motivations and is more likely to be driven by aspects of both. Ideas for research that have an initial hot motivation involve (or lead to) a desire to influence the situation that triggered our reaction. We are driven to help find a way to change the situation, so that the motivating emotion is lessened. For example, if the research idea focusses on areas such as – for example – gendered violence, racism, or corporate abuse of power, it is inevitable that we will want to try to reduce or stop these things from happening regardless of the opportunity for research. Furthermore, activism in addressing these kinds of issues is valuable and worthwhile in its own right.

To address the situations that provoke us to action *through research*, however, requires us to try to blend the hot with cold. We need to bring reflexive practices of contextualisation and conceptualisation alongside, so that we can be aware of the boundaries of the situation and decide whether and how it suggests a line of inquiry. This may be instead of or in addition to protest and activism, in some circumstances. Relationally reflexive awareness is also important as we focus on the reception of other scholarly perspectives and work out the viability of our line(s) of inquiry with others.

I think that starting hot and cooling, if I can put it that way, is sometimes easier than starting cold and trying to warm up; the drive to support change is energising. However, some will start cold and need to warm up to support their commitment to the research project. They might do so by deliberately exploring their emotional perceptions about imagined fieldwork and consider their bodies in the research context. Are there individuals or groups whose interests can be supported through the research idea? Is there anything that you feel in your gut, or your eyes (and so on) about this? Are moral emotions brought to the surface? However, there are some research projects that are purely about intellectual inquiry and people have different patterns of emotional engagement. I do not imply that these are unimportant. Nevertheless, it is worthwhile exploring all of the reflexive practices while research ideas are still forming. That kind of exploration allows us to be able to account for our motivation (as discussed above), but also provides a perspective on whether and how we can commit to a research project and remain energised throughout the execution of it.

4.3   GROUNDING IN LITERATURE

Once we understand (as well as we can) the different levels of motivation that underpin our research commitment, we need to see how this connects with others' interest in the same focal topic. The first step in this is to *ground* the project in current literature. I think it is helpful to put it that way, rather than seeking (or claiming) to systematically review the literature. This is because most studies are not based on a systematic review, but instead use a selective reading of the literature, for two reasons. If I can be forgiven the use of some rather military imagery, the two key factors underlying how we reflexively shape a focussed engagement with literature are the need to set defensive boundaries on the one hand, while at the same time pushing forward offensive boundaries on the other.

Defensive Boundaries

For many research themes the scale of the available literature can be vast, rendering it impossible to contemplate a comprehensive review in a single research project, at least in a field that focusses on journal articles to construct the research conversation. A doctoral study or a monograph can be more expansive; but many of the social sciences tend to feature longer forms of writing for integration and application, rather than for advancing new ideas that connect with current debates. Even in longer forms of writing, the risk of drowning in literature so that your own ideas sink remains an issue; it is a problem I have deliberately confronted in this book, and hope that (in this and later chapters) the lighter loading of literature is clear. In any case, the risk of being overwhelmed means that theoretical boundaries, as well as the depth of reflexive contextual engagement within those boundaries, need to be carefully considered (Hibbert, Sillince, Diefenbach & Cunliffe, 2014).

Thinking about these 'defensive' literature boundaries – largely about trying to contain a theory focus and work out the date range for limiting our engagement – involves a degree of rational reflexivity. There is a need to 'play' with alternative conceptualisations of the research focus, to find a framing that reflects our motivations but does not lead us into an overwhelming mass of literature. For this reason, we need to give an account of our position in debates in the field that reflects our world view and yet achieves some scholarly distance or perspective on the field. This still has to be *our* perspective, since:

> There is no paradigm-free, neutral position from which to choose a paradigm to work within; that is, there is no 'objective' ground for choosing a paradigm. All that one can do is work within a paradigm that is consistent with your own ultimate presumptions as a researcher... (Thompson & Perry, 2004, p. 403)

However, we need to use rational reflexivity critically, to determine whether the theoretical boundaries we set can be presented as conceptually coherent. Or to put it another way, do the boundaries make sense in the context of our implicit paradigm, once we have articulated it?

Getting from a coherent theoretical conceptualisation to an appropriate depth of historical engagement is, on one level, a matter for basic literature review skills. That is, the theoretical conceptualisation we adopt will strongly influence the appropriate time boundaries; different theoretical domains move at different rates and have different relationships to 'classic' works in the field, and this usually becomes apparent as you 'read yourself in'. On another level, there is a symbolic aspect to ensuring that the review contains material from leading publications released in the last few years. But for most of us, these rationally established limits will also be tested later in the research process, when our work is critiqued during publication revisions, bringing relational reflexive practices of reception and resolution back into the mix (Chilvers & Kearnes, 2020; Hibbert, Callagher, Siedlok, Windahl & Kim, 2019; Lupu, Spence & Empson, 2018). I will return to this point later, but for the present simply remark that the defensive boundaries we set at the outset can often turn out to be no more than 'holding patterns'.

Offensive Position

While our limits may be stretched through later relationally reflexive interactions, there is also a need to refine the defensive literature boundaries so that an argument that fits with our research motivations is supported (which is why it is important to understand those motivations first). In some ways this is another aspect of relational reflexive practice, as we turn away from inward motivation and outward to find our prospective place in the conversation with others. What do we *receive* as authoritative from published texts, and what leaves us in doubt and seeking *resolution*?

There is always some resolution to be achieved, but it depends on us shaping our turn in the literature conversation right from the start (Hibbert, Sillince, Diefenbach & Cunliffe, 2014). While we need the boundaries of our literature engagement to be defensible, we have to stay true to our motivations – so the boundaries need to seem right to us and those whose work we wish to add to or critique through our particular position. This is a question about what fits with the *argument* we are trying to make, rather than the paradigm we are *situated* in. This is where it gets complicated, because sometimes ideas from another paradigm connect well with the argument, even if their underlying frameworks might normally lead to their deliberate exclusion.

A good example is Margaret Archer's work on reflexivity (e.g., Archer, 2007), which is clearly rooted in a critical realist perspective. Although I (largely) adopt a social constructionist and interpretivist position, I still find Archer's ideas compelling and have often cited and applied them. I think this kind of manoeuvre is easiest to accomplish from an interpretivist position. The interpretivist perspective involves an expectation that the interpretation and application of material is unavoidable, with each appropriation motivated and shaped to connect to a particular conversation. Thus, I can 'interpret' critical realist (or positivist) work without being inconsistent in my approach. Mixing sources from different paradigms is less easy from some other positions; but given interpretive liberty, we can use the rational reflexive practices of contextualisation and conceptualisation to work around the problems that make it difficult to integrate ideas built on disparate foundational understandings (Alvesson, Hardy & Harley, 2008; Hibbert, Sillince, Diefenbach & Cunliffe, 2014; Collien, 2018; McLean, Harvey & Chia, 2012).

Contextualisation can be used thoughtfully to locate the ideas we want to adopt in relation to phenomena or data, rather than paradigms. For example, Archer's (2007) work has rich qualitative narratives which are very amenable to appropriation through contextualisation. By focussing on an individual's reflexivity in the context of their formative community (a strong feature of Archer's 2007 text) the ideas can be applied in ways that do not require a critical realist framing. Similarly, the conceptualisations under which these ideas are aligned can make the 'fit' with our own argument stronger; for example, by using the term 'formation' to include ideas that Archer might locate under a different label such as 'social conditioning', in work on understanding how leadership ability is developed (see Hibbert, Beech & Siedlok, 2017).

Risks in Boundary Setting and Developing a Position

Overall, the ways in which we contextualise and conceptualise literature to bring it into our argument builds our (offensive) position – the way in which we seek to impact on current debates – at the same time that it challenges our defensive limits. Moreover, there is always the possibility that reflexive practice applied to any research process can result in rejecting the notion of a concrete foundation of certain knowledge, since all researchers have their own presumptions and perspectives and each of our engagements with the literature can be *legitimately* idiosyncratic, given sufficient contextualisation. However, taken to its logical conclusion, this results in total relativism and prevents the researcher from making any useful claims at all; yes, reflexive engagement with the literature allows us to write what we want, but can we make any claims for the utility of our ideas if they are purely personal?

A pragmatic alternative position has been suggested by Parker (1995), Kilduff and Mehra (1997) and Alvesson and Skoldberg (2000), taking on board multiple views but also being open to the possibility of some degree of shareable meaning arising in the processes of interpretation. Similarly, Cunliffe (2003) suggests that in practical terms researchers need to balance transient and oppositional views with the mutually involved development of consensual meaning, if something is to be said both from and about the researched situation. Achieving this ability to speak depends on relational reflexive practice (Hibbert, Sillince, Diefenbach & Cunliffe, 2014). Arguments developed from the literature need to be exposed to critique, through reflection on texts that are (for us) authoritative and/or through exposure to conflicting views in conversation, and subsequently striving to achieve resolution. In this way, we can ensure that research building on the literature is not grounded in a self-sealed (and purely self-serving) argument.

4.4   IDENTIFICATION OF CONTEXTS

The ways in which the grounding in literature employs contextualisation to shepherd material into our argument (as discussed above) could begin the process through which the physical contexts for the research study are identified. We may well have a good idea where the themes and processes we are interested in have been studied by others or have already been experienced (to a degree) by ourselves. Conversely, however, we may have found a context first; we experience something interesting (or confronting – see the discussion of Nancy Moules' work, mentioned earlier) that has captured our attention. So, on one hand, the desired research context could be one that we begin to define through our rational (and relational) engagement with literature. However, on the other hand, it could be something that confronts us emotionally, that we notice through the reflexive practice of perception and *then* rationalise through the reflexive practices of contextualisation and conceptualisation. I am going to look at each of these alternatives in turn, before thinking about a further important question that guides context selection: namely, our anticipation of our exposure to risk in the field, on every level.

Literature-led Location of Contexts

In some cases, the literature-led location of research contexts can be obvious, or if not, then literature can at least help us to understand the importance of place and time in generating insights. At the obvious end of the spectrum, if the theme of interest is one that is clearly located in a particular kind of place, then that is where we need to be. For example, the place to study hospital management practices will obviously be hospitals and within such settings, the places and times in which those we consider to be managers are found. In contrast, if the research interest was in (say) multi-agency collaboration in the public sector, then locations may well be dispersed and hard to pin down. In addition, especially given force-majeure-driven experiences of remote, dispersed and electronically mediated social, organisational and relational arrangements, the stability and clear limits of *all* research contexts are becoming difficult to pin down.

The fluidity and porosity of research contexts, despite becoming increasingly salient in recent times, has been heralded for decades. Gille and Riain (2002), have long argued that the stability of the research site in time and space is eroding; as globalisation and virtual engagement undermines localised conceptualisations of context, more fluid, processual ideas that are focussed on flows and networks can make more sense. Even if we consider the example of hospital management mentioned earlier, then further thought identifies layers of management decision making around the institution (from the bedside to the finance department), interacting with policymakers, medical scientists and other stakeholders who shift the basis for understanding what good management can mean in terms of multiple clinical and non-clinical outcomes (Caffrey, Ferlie & McKevitt, 2019; Ferlie, Fitzgerald, Wood & Hawkins, 2005).

We may, therefore, need to have a flexible attitude to the study context, guided by contextualisation – recognising the situatedness of our experience before and during our research in any given locale – and exploring new limits suggested by our exploratory conceptualisation. In this way we can be aware of possible challenges and curiosity-driven opportunities to expand our limits, as well as considering whether there are implications for our future research practice. However, despite careful reflexive practice, the increasing fluidity of many contemporary research contexts still means that adjusting boundaries is tricky when working from a single perspective. It is difficult to see enough of the angles. Thus, involving others in challenging the initial definition of the research context, and questioning the understanding of the boundaries that then become clear, can be helpful (Hibbert, Sillince, Diefenbach & Cunliffe, 2014) and bring the reflexive practices of reception and resolution to the fore. Ultimately, the notion of a clearly bounded study site may not always be sustained. Combining data from multiple sites and times might give us more confidence in our ability to provide a better understanding of the phenomenon of interest, as it becomes evident in our interpretations (Gille & Riain, 2002).

Dealing with the uncertain and emergent boundaries of our research site(s) leads to a need to consider the length of engagement in the field, which may also be difficult to define precisely at the outset. The popularity of interview-based research is one response to this; rounds of interviews can be conducted over any period of time (within reason) and with a loosely structured framework. The focus of the research can expand, change or re-focus as insights develop (even if it is not always reported in that way) in order to deal with emerging themes or practical resource limits.

For research based in whole or part on observation in the field, a tension in the choice between long-term and short-term interventions opens up. Diachronic *and* synchronic dimensions – including an historical grounding and extended engagement alongside intensive research at a particular time – have both been argued to be important for interpretive research of this kind and there are some good arguments in favour of this stance (Vinten, 1994; Prasad, 2002; Pettigrew, 2003). Too little temporal extension and we can't really see how the phenomenon of interest came to be important in the context. Too much temporal extension and we lose the richness of an intense focus on activities and processes, which could otherwise help us and our readers to have the feeling of 'being there'. One possible balance is to have an iterative approach, translating the time boundary challenge into a series of smaller challenges across a series of linked research contexts over time (Kock, 2004).

Examples from the literature that are close to our chosen focus may help us to square the circle on all of these issues, because we will not have been the first to handle such tensions. In effect, scholars offer themselves as interlocutors through the literature. Addressing issues and practical concerns in this way is not a matter of following a recipe, but instead about engaging with the conversation offered by the literature, through the reflexive practices of reception and resolution. The focus of our (internal) conversation then becomes: what approaches to the identification of context(s) do we find challenging, and how do we resolve those difficulties through conversation with other trusted authors? Starting out, we often give methodology textbooks that trusted place, but as research experience grows, we may instead look to particular communities and insights from recent studies.

Emotionally Led Location of Contexts: Following Hot Motivations

It may seem that, in the discussion of the literature-led identification of research contexts, I have made the process seem more difficult than it needs to be. Perhaps that is so; but as we turn to emotionally led identification of contexts, it may be the case that I balance that out, by leading you to think that the emotionally led route to the selection of research contexts is too simple a process. In some ways it *is* simple, since it is likely driven by a 'hot motivation' (as discussed earlier) for the research study. Being motivated by – say – outrage at injustice is rooted in powerful experiences, rather than being an abstract theoretical question; for that reason it leads to a laser-like focus on the context(s) in which the injustice was observed. A good example of this is described by Stringer and Simmons (2015, p. 253):

> We found disturbing cases of human rights abuses, when 7 Indonesian crew members from the Shin Ji, a South Korean foreign charter vessel (FCV), refused to work, citing physical and sexual abuse, as well as the non-payment of wages. They were followed a month later by 32 Indonesian crew members from the Oyang 75, another South Korean vessel. Shocked by the accounts of horrific inhumane working conditions on board these vessels, we decided to look further into the FCV sector.

The perception of emotions – feeling disturbed and shocked – is rapidly combined in reflexive practice here with contextualisation to focus on the issue in the sector, rather than in other contexts where oppression between national groups might be found. I think that this also fulfils a rational criterion (if it needs to): the phenomenon of modern slavery, one of the long-term focusses of Stringer and Simmons' work, is clearly evident in the context. However, their focus also reflected their emotional engagement with the particular suffering individuals that they encountered. As I will relate later in this section, this turned out to be a troubling and difficult context to research. To be clear, Stringer and Simmons (2015) do not explicitly discuss reflexive practice around the perception of their emotions (research conventions often drive us towards articulating detachment), but there is a strong current of moral emotion throughout their work. I think this is important, since it underscores the importance of carefully considering our perceptions of emotion when it is pulling us towards a context. Moral outrage seems like 'good anger', an emotion that we might choose to follow whereas (say) contempt might not be such a good guide towards an important research context. It is undeniably a personal preference, but I think that emotions that arise from sympathy for the plight of others are a much better guide for research (and re-orienting ourselves through reflexive practice) than emotions that are associated with seeing others as worth less than ourselves. What I mean here is to consider the different angles for approaching the same theme. For example, choosing to focus on the plight of an oppressed minority and their needs, rather than adopting a laser-like focus on the demonisation of oppressors. Starting from either point may eventually get us to the same place, but we are more likely to shape our work in ways that make a difference (and perhaps gather support) with the former approach.

There is an exception to my moral rule-of-thumb though, and that relates to autoethnographic research. Focussing on the perception of our emotions when they are driving us towards a particular context does not mean that we are trying to diminish our presence in the research in favour of others, but rather to orient ourselves within it, to *then* be able to say something that is useful for others (Hibbert, Beech, Callagher & Siedlok, 2021). If our attention is specifically directed *inwards* in autoethnographic work, then even the most 'unworthy' emotions can lead to an account that helps others be honest about their difficult emotions too. Autoethnographies should be the most emotionally involved, innately reflexive contexts for research and it is tempting to say that if the protagonist emerges without fault, then it will not have the ring of authenticity. For example, Clarke's (2017) account of collating good memories of his relationship with his father, as he works through his grief after his father's death from cancer, has the moving ring of authenticity. Even good memories are still tinged with regret:

> The cottage where I live, Fliskmillan, Newburgh, Cupar, Fife, Scotland. I live at the bottom of a very steep hill in prime farming territory, overlooking the River Tay, in North Fife. My Dad loved it here. He came to visit twice. On both occasions, as soon as he got out of the car, I reminded him, just as we had agreed on the telephone before his arrival:
>> This is a non-smoking house. All smoking is to be done outside. And not right outside the front, or back door. Go around the side of the house where there are no windows with air vents!
> During his second visit, I remember asking, "Dad, how do you find it up here, in Scotland?" Thinking about it now, speaking to him like that, the way I did, I wonder why he even bothered visiting me…?! (Clarke, 2017, p. 475)

This prelude makes the following tiny conversation between Daniel (Clarke) and his father all the more poignant:

> "Well, it's ideal isn't it…?!"
>> What do you like about it?" I quizzed.
> "I love the sound of the wind rustling through the trees.
>> It's like music! It's strong! It doesn't sound like that in Kirkby."
>> Maybe I didn't make him feel as welcome as I could have. Perhaps I didn't need to say it like I did. Next time I … (Clarke, 2017, p. 475)

Emotion led Clarke into his griefwork, and his perception of his emotions helps him to tell stories in ways that others who have had difficult relationships with their fathers can find meaningful. That includes me: I thought about the small stories that Clarke tells a lot, and while I didn't recover so many positive incidents in my own case, there were perhaps some glimpses. What is also interesting from that kind of emotional identification of context is that, while the temporal sweep can be very broad (a whole lifetime, in Clarke's case) the physical context of a particular incident can be extraordinarily precise. Clarke's home address gives some indication of this, but there is more in his article (Clarke, 2017).

Overall, I do not think that emotional identification of contexts *needs* more than the emotional reflexive practice of perception to guide it, since it can have both breadth and precision, but there is an almost instinctual link to rational reflexive practices of contextualisation and conceptualisation. That link leads to questions such as: Can I locate and describe this feeling coherently? How can I frame what I say about it in this situation in this context, in ways others find useful? Answers to these questions are partly resolved in interpretive analysis and partly resolved in the writing, through different reflexive practices. I will return to these questions later.

Contexts and (Reflexive) Risks

The emotionally driven selection of contexts overlaps a great deal with 'hot' motivation for a research study. 'Selecting' a research context in this way can have certain dangers. We are likely to commit to placing ourselves in the midst of a situation where there might be some risks to the viability of the research and even – and more importantly – our safety. Stringer and Simmons (2015, p. 257) give an account of how frightening situations can result from these risks:

> One evening, a direct confrontation occurred, when Indonesian crew members from one South Korean vessel and two of our translators accompanied us to dinner, following a meeting with government officials. [...] By chance, the crew members' former employer and his wife were dining at the same restaurant as us. During dinner, some of the people who had participated in our study became agitated as the wife of their former employer took photos of them and made phone calls. They then noticed a second employer and his associates waiting outside the restaurant. [...] As we left the restaurant, both former New Zealand employers as well as three of their associates were waiting for us. [...] We were stalked and photographed, and our vehicles were followed which forced us to take a series of evasive manoeuvres over the next hour to lose them.

Stringer and Simmons' (2015) work was located in a particularly risky context, but that is the kind of situation that moral outrage is likely to lead us into. I am certainly not suggesting that we should avoid such dark places: they need to have light shone on them. But we do need to think about how our reflexive practice will help us to cope with the strain and help us to realise if and when to stop. I think that relational reflexive practices, involving trusted colleagues, are really important in these cases. We need others to look out for us. The risks of research in contexts in which we are emotionally invested are not just related to dangers such as intimidation, as outlined above. Any personal engagement – especially in autoethnography (Boncori & Smith, 2019; Davies, McGregor & Horan, 2019; Fernando, Reveley & Learmonth, 2020) – can leave us with a burden that we have to resolve through later reflexive practice with others. A later segment in Clarke's (2017) article helps to make this clear:

> After remembering, then, the mundane moments with my dad when he was at his best, what am I left with? While these beautiful moments have been preserved, a darkness cast by the shadows that remain lives on inside me. (Clarke, 2017, p. 476)

Of course, this does not mean that I am advocating literature-led location of contexts in preference to emotion-led location of contexts. You will have been aware how much attention I have given to the latter in comparison to the former, a choice which you will interpret for yourself. However, it is also important to point out that literature-led approaches are not without risk either. Being too conservative and careful can mean studies are far less interesting than those where the researchers are clearly personally invested. Overall, it is likely that we will achieve a balance between these two ways of locating our research contexts, mediated through rational and relational reflexive practice.

4.5   CHOICES ABOUT DATA COLLECTION

Interpretive studies require pragmatic approaches for gathering material that reflects the complex challenges and choices set out above. We need to collate material that addresses our motivations, connects with our early literature-based theoretical position and ensures that the locations we select – bounded in time and space – provide us with opportunities to access those we wish to engage or observe (or most likely both).

There are additional layers of complexity that are added when we reflect in more depth on the nature of qualitative data, especially in field research involving ethnographic approaches based on participant observation (Beech, Hibbert, McInnes & MacIntosh, 2009; Cunliffe & Karunanayake, 2013; Grahle & Hibbert, 2020; Rosen, 2019). Data in such cases may stretch across presumed or desired levels of analysis (conceptually and temporally) and require thoughtful combination to provide a useful picture. With that in mind, when we think about what 'counts' as data we can find that it does not fit neatly within our original conceptual and temporal boundaries. While there are strategies for containing the complexity through a literature focus (as discussed earlier) – looking through a narrowly focussed theoretical lens – another approach is to engage reflexively with the tensions we encounter alongside the emerging conceptualisations we develop in our fieldwork. These tensions can help to expand on the discussion of the fluidity of research contexts that I set out earlier, and one way of framing them is to consider the balance between observation and engagement, and then reconsider the balance between short- and long-term participation in research contexts.

There is a clear tension between observation and engagement. Many of the phenomena or systems explored in interpretive research are often complex, dynamic and contingent. Furthermore, the problem of tacit knowing (Polanyi, 1966) – people knowing more than they can say – also applies here. This means that the research participants may not explicate their understanding of the situation(s) in ways that can be communicated easily in field interviews. In addition to which, while both research participants and researchers may feel that they are approaching a good, mutual understanding, our biases and performative intentions in communication can be expected to influence what is shared and a certain degree of criticality is called for (Alvesson, 2003; Wilson, 2004).

The problems involved in direct communication favour non-participatory research approaches, such as observational work (Grahle & Hibbert, 2020). However, Lichterman (1998) suggests that participation is as important as observation. In addition, Heracleous (2001) has argued that participation by the researcher can lead to additional inferences, as 'subject reactivity' yields new data through participant reactions to both the message and the messenger (the actively participating researcher). There are, however, possible risks in over-emphasising action if the balance of the research is tipped too far towards participation, perhaps leading to emotionally over-committed positions – *very* hot motivations – or distracting engagement in political manoeuvring (Pettigrew, 2003; Kock, 2004). As Weeks (2000) suggests, a possible balance point is to be engaged *enough* to be able to develop informed interpretations about what is observed.

Setting aside autoethnographic approaches, a position in which there are boundaries to participation in the situation may often be an appropriate stance. In this way the connection to less obvious levels of understanding may be possible, without the risk of generating overly action-oriented, context bound findings (Ayas, 2003). Consider, for example, about how Stringer and Simmons (2015) developed an engaged, balanced position; they went on to generate critical and generalisable insights about modern slavery, while still caring deeply about the situation of their study participants. Overall, a balance between observation and participation is best achieved through relational reflexive practice, establishing a good-enough connection with participants to receive new insights, and resolving the difficulties in connecting those insights with our established ideas through dialogue (Chilvers & Kearnes, 2020; Cunliffe, 2002; Hibbert, Callagher, Siedlok, Windahl & Kim, 2019; Hibbert, Sillince, Diefenbach & Cunliffe, 2014; Kogler, 1999).

There is also a tension between short- and long-term engagement in research contexts. On the one hand this can be a practical concern – we cannot always spend the time that we would like in the field – but on the other hand, there are also issues that require some rational reflexive practice in order to be resolved. Contextualisation can illuminate how our own history is involved in arriving at interpretations in the field (Collien, 2018; McLean, Harvey & Chia, 2012; Sklaveniti & Steyaert, 2020) but there is a similar depth of history for others in the field too. We need to be attentive to the reflexive practice of concep-tualisation (Alvesson, Hardy & Harley, 2008; Hibbert, Sillince, Diefenbach & Cunliffe, 2014), asking if and how the emerging concepts in our studies suggest the depth of history of research participants, and not just our own hinterland. Galibert (2004, p. 456) suggests that a central question is "How can we be astonished by what is most familiar, and make familiar what is strange?"

A good example here relates to assumptions around commonplace terms; for example, 'childcare' means quite different things to those looking from an educational, social work or policing background (Huxham & Vangen, 2005). This can mean that one signal of having spent enough time in the field is that the emerging concepts provide a degree of surprise – we arrive at an impression that there is more going on than we expected, rather than finding our common-sense views to be enough. There is no formula for an appropriate length of engagement to allow such impressions to develop, although they can go alongside the development of trusting relationships with participants (Beech, Hibbert, McInnes & MacIntosh, 2009), be accelerated by background research (Vinten, 1994) or made more feasible through multiple short cycles of engagement in the field over time (Gille & Riain, 2002; Kock, 2004).

4.6   APPROACHES TO ANALYSIS AND GENERATING SHAREABLE INSIGHTS

There is a huge range of material on the formal analysis of qualitative data already available in textbooks, training courses, and specialised journals (see, especially, *Organisational Research Methods*). It is beyond the scope and purpose of this book to engage with that breadth, although I touch on some points in later case study chapters (Chapters 5 and 6). Instead, I want to focus on some particular challenges for the reflexive researcher engaged in interpretive work. For us, analysis is always already ongoing in the process of collecting data. As discussed above, this unavoidable interpretive work helps us to know when we have engaged in the field enough to be able to have something of interest to write about our focal topic. But it also provides a generative space in which the future content of our writing begins to take shape. As analytical processes continue away from the field and feed into the processes of formal writing and revision (Hibbert, Sillince, Diefenbach & Cunliffe, 2014), two new challenges arise. The first challenge relates to deciding about writing ourselves *in* or *out* of the interpreted data, bearing in mind that in much of our experience in the field we are personally engaged – emotional and embodied – rather than neutral intellectual observers. The second, overlapping challenge relates to balancing authentic representations of what we have learned with setting out some generalised or generalisable insights that make our work relevant to others.

There are different possibilities in addressing the two challenges, one of which was addressed in Chapter 2: choosing between writing accounts in an engaged or an objective style. This leads to one particular option that seems to solve both challenges at once, by moving the lever all the way across the scale towards objectivity and generalisability. However, as discussed earlier, that objectively oriented approach limits full engagement with reflexive practice. The other extreme – shifting the lever back the other way – is autobiography, in which the research experience is simply an aspect of the researcher's life and recorded as such. While autobiography may touch and resonate with readers, it does not seek to offer generalised insights. It does, however, suggest a middle way: the use of narrative forms that are designed to engage readers in an experience of specific insights. This approach still tilts towards authenticity and resonance, but it has scope that stretches beyond this.

Despite the aesthetic challenge of narratives that tends to particularise them – crafting them in a way that is interesting, their inherent dependency on a particular setting and possibilities for multiple and uncertain meanings – they have been argued to have value as a means of *thoughtful* generalisation (Kearney, 2002). Although others might raise objections to the use of narratives in that way (Langley, 1999; Abell, 2004), a 'middle of the road' position is possible by thinking differently about what is meant by generalisation. Arguably, generalisation is about the way we manage the integration of 'emerging' theory, in terms of broad connections, into the domains of 'accepted' theory and practice. Most often in qualitative research this is most achieved through a synthetic (Langley, 1999) approach of identifying core thematic elements. But even in such cases, narrative can still have a role through the use of 'micro-stories' (Boje, Luhman & Baack, 1999). Micro-stories may be illustrative data quotes from those used in inductively developing themes or building theory. Micro-stories can give the flavour of a particular process, locate a pivotal and revelatory incident or help to show the depth of the hinterland behind some particular captured conversation or observation.

Paradoxically, micro-stories both give rise to and help to overcome the charge of anecdotalism that has been levelled at some interpretive research (Wilson, 2004). However, the value of micro-stories lies in the way in which they provide a 'feel' for the reality of the conveyed theory, allow multiple perspectives to be retained and transmitted, and provide the necessary authenticity that makes research accounts convincing (Golden-Biddle & Locke, 1993). Going further, including our own micro-stories can help to give more confidence in the work by explicating our own role and influence in the process (Wiley, 1987). This self-inclusion in narrative and micro-story forms also provides a particular place for capturing embodied reflexive practice, noticed through interoception. It also provides a way of capturing our emotional reflexive practice when it would neutralise the data to exclude these perceptions, as in the example of the dangers faced by Stringer and Simmons (2015), discussed earlier. Another good example of these points is offered in the work of Purnell and Clarke (2019), which connects to and builds on Clarke's (2017) account of his relationship with his father that was discussed earlier:

David [Purnell]:
My mother tried to have me interact with my father as a child. I ask my mother for permission to go to a friend's house, and she directs me to ask my father. I never

ask; I'm too scared. When I was forced to interact with my father, it was awkward; neither of us knew how to do that dance. I want and don't want to talk to my father. Embarrassment, fear, and love fight it out silently along every neural pathway from my brain to my suddenly silent mouth. Perhaps it is easier to blame my father, than to forgive him. […]
Daniel [Clarke]:
I need to take a step back and break down the frustration I had with my father's drink-fuelled fathering. Men with alcoholic fathers often declare "I certainly don't want to be like my dad". (Purnell & Clarke, 2019, p. 912)

Purnell and Clarke go on to explore the links between their stories in a relationally reflexive step, seeking to receive what the other offers and struggling to resolve the tensions that follow:

These emotionally charged memories twist and intertwine themselves into each other's narrative forming not a bow, but a knot. We are left with a knot in ourselves from resolved/not resolved issues with our fathers. We are left with knots in our narratives as the tellings become blurred as to their authorship. (Purnell & Clarke, 2019, p. 913)

The accounts of close, damaged and damaging relationships make Purnell and Clarke's (2019) account a particularly good example of the use of micro-stories. While applying the same style to other research settings – for example organisational contexts – might seem more difficult, all of our research sites contain embodied and emotional individuals, not least ourselves. However, understanding what might be generalisable from our embedding in the data does require some rational and relational reflexivity, to work out our connections and impact within the research (Callagher, El Sahn, Hibbert, Korber & Siedlok, 2021; Heracleous, 2001; Humphreys, Brown & Hatch, 2003; Kogler, 1999). This implies caution in relation to the claims we generate, entertaining the necessary reflexive 'hermeneutics of doubt' (Prasad, 2002), whilst not giving way to spiralling uncertainty (Cunliffe, 2003). A common approach to anchoring our research claims in order to accommodate both insights and doubt is to reconnect to extant literature, as discussed below.

4.7 RECONNECTING TO LITERATURE: WRITING INTO A CONVERSATION

In the processes of developing insights from interpretive research, we face all of the complexity of the theory building process that Langley records in her (1999) work on process research. All interpretive research generally has similar layers of complexity; inductive and deductive elements are often combined, and some degree of creativity seems to be essential. Focussing this creative aspect through reconnection with literature helps us to make sure that our contribution joins a conversation, in ways that can be heard and understood. Both rational and relational modes of reflexive practice are involved in this process.

The accounts we generate are both embedded in and descriptive of the situations that have been researched, and the rationally reflexive practices of contextualisation (turned in this case on the hinterland of our research participants as well as ourselves, as mentioned earlier) and conceptualisation are important, although the balance we strike might lean more on one practice than the other, depending on our motivations which can lead us towards leaning more towards generalisability or authenticity. If we are seeking to provide a descriptive theory that is close to the context and experience of participants, we are likely to choose a narrative form focussed on a particular case. It is a common complaint that such approaches offer limited insights for others in different circumstances (Abell, 2004). Against such positions it can be argued that each reader will interpret material into their own framework of understanding in any case (Heracleous, 2001; Hibbert, Beech & Siedlok, 2017; Sklaveniti & Steyaert, 2020) making prescriptive, 'scientific' approaches inappropriate or ineffective.

By reconnecting our accounts with extant literature, we provide additional framing that places boundaries around the conceptualisations that our reflexive practice provides, within the context of the narrative. This allows readers interpretive freedom to appropriate our insights in their own context, but to do so within the horizons of current debate (Vandevelde, 2010). That is, we encourage readers to join the conversation in the same way that we ourselves do, by opening up the potential for a fusion of horizons (Chilvers & Kearnes, 2020; Gadamer, 1998; Hibbert, Beech & Siedlok, 2017) within which the possibility of (imperfect) mutual understanding arises. In other words, literature citations can serve as boundary markers to help encourage others along the same path with us, by allowing them to engage their apperception (contextualisation and conceptualisation) to connect our understandings with their own situations and issues.

However, connecting the insights from our reflexive practices of conceptualisation and contextualisation with ideas from existing literature does not always lead to closure. Rational apperception only takes readers so far and they instead enter into the relational reflexive practices of receiving and resolving; however, sometimes this leaves viable competing interpretations in play. In some ways, keeping options open and in play leads to more possible ways of connecting with the reader. The research approach of my retired colleague Chris Huxham was centred on explicating these multiple possibilities at the micro-level and avoiding *pre-emptive* closure (see Huxham & Hibbert, 2011, for an overview of the approach and a connection to her wider work) and this can be a way of enabling others to share our angle on the conversation while keeping alternatives open. The space for connecting and challenging is widened through the presentation of competing interpretations (Kilduff & Mehra, 1997; Boje, Luhman & Baack, 1999) which may also be a good reflection of the intrinsic complexity of the situation. There may be a case for looser ties to the anchors of literature in order to retain this openness, especially when allied to alternative forms of writing. Producing work in (what we hope will be received as) literary genres means that readers will engage with the material differently; we sidestep the constraints of anchoring in literature but encounter the need to satisfy aesthetic criteria – and current critical opinion – instead (Humphreys, Brown & Hatch, 2003).

Overall, we have choices in relation to how we connect with literature with a number of aims in mind, and with different balances of reflexive practices. Importantly, we need to consider readers engaging in reflexive practice as they pick up our work. They meet us relationally in the text, ready to receive what we offer and engage in their own rational reflexive practices of contextualisation and conceptualisation (Hibbert, Sillince, Diefenbach & Cunliffe, 2014; Collien, 2018; McLean, Harvey & Chia, 2012) to build a connection, returning to the text with a possibility for closure and resolution where this introduces tensions, or keeping multiple possibilities open where this is necessary or helpful. It is most likely that the more challenging the ideas offered, the greater the degree of openness that will be retained. Even where some precision is possible, we can expect each reader to arrive, via their own traditions and history, at their own interpretation in any case; we can only hope to provide some possibilities for connecting our interpretation with theirs within a shared horizon of understanding (Gadamer, 1998; Hibbert, Siedlok & Beech, 2016; Hibbert, Beech & Siedlok, 2017).

4.8   RESPONDING TO CRITIQUE

Despite all of the careful reflexive practice that may underlie the accounts of our research, our ambition to join an intellectual conversation will usually be challenged in the process of (seeking) publication. While the range of ways of communicating online that can sidestep peer review is increasing, I don't usually recommend these alternatives. Instead, there are two reasons for accepting (what often feels like) the difficult struggle of peer review. The first is that the outlets that have strong review processes tend to be those with the highest standing and larger readerships (and, pragmatically or cynically, are most recognised at career review points like promotion or tenure). So, if one's work is intended to make a difference to others as well as yourself through academic conversation, peer-reviewed outlets are likely to be the best choice. The second and more important reason is that peer review opens up an exploratory space in which you can see if readers are engaging with your ideas in the ways that you expected... or whether their reflexive practices of reception and resolution (Chilvers & Kearnes, 2020; Hibbert, Callagher, Siedlok, Windahl & Kim, 2019; Lupu, Spence & Empson, 2018) leave them with unresolved issues that they turn back to you, leaving you with further work of contextual-isation and conceptualisation (Hibbert, Sillince, Diefenbach & Cunliffe, 2014; Collien, 2018; McLean, Harvey & Chia, 2012) to undertake. Our ideas may be stretched in helpful ways through cycles of relationally reflexive interactions like this. However, an awareness of the uncertainties in that process underlines why we seek to establish our position in the conversation right from the start through connections with extant research and tie our insights back to this body of work, when we are shaping our contribution (Hibbert, Sillince, Diefenbach & Cunliffe, 2014).

We also, though, have to stay true to our motivations, especially when they are 'hot' and strongly driven by emotional perceptions. If you are personally invested in your work to the degree that you find critique invasive – to the point that you may literally 'feel it in your guts' through interoceptive aware-ness – then your choice may be to choose a form or route that leaves more of you on the pages and respects your pain. For example, the journal *Qualitative Inquiry* is not one that colleagues in Daniel Clarke's discipline often publish in, but it allows authors to preserve their unique voice and personal insights (see Clarke, 2017; Purnell & Clarke, 2019) in the way that other outlets might not. However, it is also important to recognise that even if our motivations are cold (or cooling) then we will likely still feel a sting from any critique, simply because of the time commitment and sense of self that are tied up in research and writing. This should not lead us to seek alternative outlets until we have at least let the emotions arising from critique settle, before looking at the review again with a cooler view. There needs to be an acknowledgement of the emotional perceptions that follow from our investment in our work. With that acknowledgement in place, it is possible to move on to the rounds of relational and rational reflexive practice involved in developing our work in the (awk-wardly anonymous) collaborative environment of peer review.

4.9   OVERVIEW

The necessary steps involved in interpretive research can be both planned and emergent with, as I have argued above, a complex array of reflexive practices that are involved, whether these are acknowledged or not. That is, some reflexive practices are involved deliberately and some less so, in the process of completing a particular study. While emphasising, again, that the process may not be as linear or tidy as the preceding discussion, I think it is useful to summarise how reflexive practices are useful across the lifetime of a study. These insights are summarised in Table 4.1.

Table 4.1   *Reflexive practices foregrounded in research processes*

Element of the research process	Reflexive practices that are foregrounded
Characterisation and commitment	Developing a research idea: commitment to it tends to involve rational reflexive (contextualisation and conceptualisation) practices and relational reflexive (reception and resolution) practices if the motivation is *cold* (literature driven). For *hot* motivation (personally significant projects), ideas will instead be driven by emotional and embodied reflexive practices (perception and interoception). Projects will likely be shaped by aspects of both motivations, over time.
Grounding in literature	Both 'defensive' boundaries and an 'offensive' position (how we choose to push the limits) in relation to a literature review are established with the help of rational reflexive practices. Balancing the risk of being too conservative on the one hand or on the other hand pushing limits too far, requires relational reflexive practice.
Identification of contexts	For predominantly *cold* motivated projects, establishing suitable research contexts involves rational reflexive practices, with issues of complexity addressed through relational reflexive practices. For predominantly *hot* motivated projects, emotional reflexive practices will lead more-or-less directly to the contexts we are drawn to study. However, rational reflexive practices can help to ensure that we will be able to generate insights from these contexts. *Hot* motivations and being guided into contexts by emotional reflexive practices can carry some risks, so care is needed.
Choices about data collection	Reflexive practice is useful in helping to establish the appropriate boundaries for data collection in two ways. Relational reflexive practice, through engagement with participants, helps to identify the spatial boundaries for (e.g.,) participant observation. Rational reflexive practice helps to establish the time limits for engagement: when we have a sense that our contextualisation has been sufficiently enriched by participants and our conceptualisations have been expanded in unexpected ways.
Approaches to analysis and generating shareable insights	Narrative formats or the use of 'micro-stories' can help to preserve the insights from emotional and embodied reflexive practice in the field. Some engagement with rational and relational reflexive practice is necessary in finding ways to share the full range of insights in conceptualisations that can be understood (well enough) by others and have some utility for them.
Reconnecting to literature and readers: writing into a conversation	A complex interplay of rational and relational reflexive practice – treating cited authors as distanced partners in dialogue – is necessary to establish the possibility of a 'fusion of horizons' in which there is space for a contribution to debates/conversations to be understood.
Responding to critique	Cycles of relational and rational reflexive practice are involved in reshaping our texts in response to critique, with the caveat that we may reach limits that would prevent us speaking with an authentic voice. Emotional and embodied reflexive practice may signal if and when those limits are reached.

While the table shows how particular reflexive practices are foregrounded in particular phases of the research, it is important to bear in mind two caveats. First, all of the types of reflexive practice are potentially active at any time. The discussion in this chapter and the summaries in the table are intended to show where our focus is *likely* to be, in that particular part of the process. Although emotions and embodiment are the levels of reflexivity that are the least discussed, these aspects of ourselves do not go away and may surface at any time. Such surfacing may signal an important insight just out of reach, or simply reflect our daily life, health and (most often, sadly) levels of stress. It is important to pay attention to the significant emotional perceptions and interoceptive insights that arise at any time, to consider what they may be signalling.

Second, research is seldom a neat, linear process and some approaches are deliberately cyclical. Rather than research phases, the headings in this chapter can be seen as principal research activities, which may be combined and blended in different ways. For example, especially in doctoral work, writing is a constant practice; we contextualise and conceptualise in our writing as we go, whether we wish to or not. Capturing (at least) significant insights from our reflexive practice in a parallel text – often a research diary – can help us to sort out the picture that is already emerging, long before we expected it.

Dialogue

1. I have described 'hot' and 'cold' motivations for engaging in research. How does that connect with your experience of emotional and intellectual engagement in your research study(s)?
2. In the progress of a research project, there are more choices, risks and trade-offs than we might first expect. How does reflexive practice play a role in how you manage these in issues?
3. The reflexive practices that will be foregrounded in particular research phases may not be the same in every context or for every researcher. How might you expect your pattern of reflexive practices to vary from my picture?

5. Case study: reflexive practice in PhD research

Just after the end of my PhD I was working on a possible journal paper with my former doctoral supervisor/advisor,[1] Chris. I had built up some confidence (and developed my own opinions!) by then, and sometimes our discussions were quite... robust. We were arguing about the literature section of the paper.
Chris: "You have missed all the details here. [Paper X] is not only about that theme, [Paper Y] could also suggest another concept, [Paper Z] has relevance in two other ways [...and so on...] – we need about 15 themes if we are going to capture all of the details of the literature!"
Me: "I am not trying to capture all of the bloody details, I am trying to corral it into three themes so that we can write something without drowning in bloody concepts!"
There was a pause, in which it dawned on both of us that this had been the tension between our approaches for years, and that was the first time that I had voiced it...

5.1 LEARNING TO JOIN THE CONVERSATION

It is something of a commonplace understanding these days to think of a doctoral degree as an apprenticeship, at the end of which you would be confident to take your own position in the academy and be able to argue competently with your (former) PhD supervisor. My experiences in the 'doctoral apprenticeship' certainly helped me to learn to argue. The doctoral program was also a time of tremendous reflexive learning and change in many directions, not all of which were focussed on the development of a thesis.

The need to implement reflexivity in interpretive doctoral research is key. It is important not just in terms of producing a good thesis, but also in terms of understanding how we make choices and develop through the degree program. The primary choice was established in Chapter 2, where I indicated that there are two ways of implementing reflexivity in particular research projects, depending on whether we choose to focus on generalisability or on authenticity and resonance. This chapter and Chapter 6, therefore, provide case study illustrations of how reflexive practice plays out in relation to either of those aims. In this first case study, my doctoral research provides an example in which the intention was to maximise generalisability. That is, to where the intention was, as set out in Chapter 2, to:

> Maximise the generalisability of the understandings generated [by the researcher] in their projects, by eliminating the influence of their situated interpretive stance, as much as that is possible.

In most doctoral research, which requires the demonstration of a unique contribution to knowledge, generalisability is usually a presumed aim.[2] The most appropriate example I can work with to illustrate how this reflexivity supports this is my own doctoral study (completed many years ago), since it allows me to comment on reflexive practice 'from the inside' with an awareness of embodied, emotional, rational and relational levels. I also think that looking at what goes on in a doctoral study is useful for three particular reasons.

First, every doctoral supervisor will tell you that there is no such thing as a perfect PhD, only a finished one. In using my work as an illustration, I will prove this common wisdom to be true; but the mistakes we make can often help us to realise (sometimes long after the event) where reflexive practice could have made a difference then and can help us in the future.

Second, doctoral studies often employ a breadth of theory, along with a depth of fieldwork and data collection, that may be difficult to sustain in later projects when the responsibilities of an academic career are multiplying. In my case, although my research focussed on an organisational studies problem, the findings were deeply rooted in sociological theory and the approach was based on extensive participant observation over a number of years (which also means that my study has similarities to many beyond the confines of my own specialised field). However, I will not be delving into the study's theoretical debates or findings in any depth, except where particular points, which support an understanding of the application of reflexive practice, can best be illuminated through the use of illustrative material.

Third, doctoral studies often include choices, changes of direction and other layers of complexity that other studies may not. This makes them good sites for illustrating issues that may not be so obvious in simpler projects. For example, my doctoral research had an unusual structure and a non-standard approach to analysis. I am not offering it as a template for how to go about completing a doctorate (the unusual analytical approach meant that it was harder than it needed to be, to be honest, and involved unnecessary challenges in developing the material for later publication). However, my experience does illustrate a wide range of difficulties that may be encountered by others and how reflexive practice can help to address those challenges.

It is helpful to set out the basic context of my doctoral research at this point, in order to locate the experiences I discuss below. I completed my study at the University of Strathclyde, in Scotland, between 2001 and 2005. I started part-time, but in the last year or so of the process I was lucky enough to secure a research fellowship. I came to doctoral study in an unconventional way, having spent time in industry and after studying an MBA at Strathclyde's Graduate School of Business. At that time the Graduate School featured both a high-ranking program and high-profile, interesting (and in some cases unconventional) academic staff who were actively recruiting doctoral students. The Graduate School was dissolved and integrated into a broader faculty structure in the years that followed.

Having established the purpose of the chapter and briefly explained the context of my doctoral program, the rest of the chapter is arranged as follows. I first step through each of the phases discussed in Chapter 4, explaining how reflexive practice was involved in that phase as I experienced it in my doctoral program. In doing so I highlight some missed opportunities and show how, in some ways, the phases can be blurred and approached iteratively. I then summarise the patterns of reflexive practice (present and absent) in the study and explore how I might have approached doctoral research differently, while drawing out speculative advice for other doctoral students and those who guide them.

5.2   CHARACTERISATION, MOTIVATIONS AND COMMITMENT

My initial research project was loosely framed around an interest in "what makes collaboration work?" I was able to start with such a broad question because it was a close fit with my doctoral supervisor's interests and approach. Chris Huxham had already established a long, empirically grounded program of research focussed on inter-organisational collaboration, which focussed on how collaborative advantage (Huxham & Vangen, 2005) was made possible or obstructed when organisations worked together on joint projects or programs. Her approach was based on cycles of participant observation and an open, interpretive engagement with data (see Huxham & Hibbert, 2011). The idea was to engage with practitioners who were trying to make collaboration work, notice themes that regularly occurred and then focus on those topics in more detail. Thus, it is possible to see my position within this existing program of research as being driven by cold motivation. There was an existing and rich body of work taking diverse perspectives on the phenomenon (there is an extensive community of researchers interested in inter-organisational collaboration and how it works – see, for example, Hibbert, Huxham and Ring (2008), for an indication of the breadth that is still valid). There was also an expectation that new themes could be identified in field research, if I took care to be aware of the main themes the literature had already covered.

I would never encourage a doctoral student to start their research in such a loose way! There was no articulation of a clear 'gap' in the literature or the adoption of a problematising theory lens. Added to which, the practice context where I was seeking to make a difference was far too broad – it could include public–private partnerships, public sector joint initiatives, professional networks, international alliances and many other forms, all of which could be described as inter-organisational collaborations. There were imbalances in reflexive practice that I can now recognise – and will explore below – in the start-up of my research that account for my decision to proceed with such a poorly defined project. However, to be kind to my (somewhat) younger self, I want to point out that my understanding of reflexivity and reflexive practice would only develop (partly through a specific 'side project') across the course of my doctoral studies. In addition to which, there are always things that are only recognised in the rear-view mirror.

One of the shaping imbalances related to the dynamic between relational reflexive practice and rational reflexive practice. For someone entering an academic career on a non-standard trajectory (after an industry career), the degree of reliance on the supervisor as a guide to an unfamiliar world is high. My relational reflexive practice of reception was strong in the early days; I took on board Chris' advice and more-or-less considered it to be normative. There was not much need for the practice of resolution – fitting another's ideas into your own frameworks and working through the tensions – because I didn't think that my own experience had any relevance. Instead, I thought that my responsibility was to build a new framework from the ground up, although this sometimes made the new intellectual tools feel distant and alien. However, I had some experience of research in other paradigms during my industry career, which could have led me to question the lack of focus when starting out and led me to explore debates and different approaches. I could have brought to bear the rational reflexive practices of contextualisation and conceptualisation to the framing of the project, to understand how I could make sense of it in a way that connected to my earlier experience and made more immediate sense... and then take the results of that back to supervisor discussions. That kind of process happened more often later, albeit without a formal understanding of the reflexive practices at the time.

The other shaping imbalance was possibly more important; it was concerned with a lack of attention to emotional and embodied reflexive practices. The emotional angle was important on many levels, not least the initial (but later irrelevant) hot motivation for engaging in research in the first place. Here is the real back-story about that: I took up research on collaboration part-time after completing an MBA, mostly because my experience on the program had ended with an infuriating experience of collaborative work, an experience which left me boiling mad! Despite the abilities of the MBA team I was working with, the dynamics were impossible, and the work was not great. I don't want to embarrass myself and others with (what I now see) as trivial details, but I can *still* feel my gut tighten and my jaw clench when I think of it, decades later. At the time, I was strongly driven to find practical solutions that could help those kinds of problems to be avoided. Having an interest in the research topic that was strongly driven by that kind of emotional perception gave me the energy to engage, but probably contributed to a missing focus on the interplay of rational and relational reflexivity that could have sharpened the initial approach to research. That would come later.

In addition, the dynamics of becoming a PhD student after an industry career led to some other emotional perceptions that were also influential. After being a manager and completing an MBA (which, in my case at least, *did* come with the stereotypical boost of arrogance), starting out on a PhD felt diminishing. As a fellow student who started around the same time, after having a leading role in a charitable organisation, remarked: "we're plankton". These kinds of feelings were not precipitated through any unkindness from supervisors or the other established scholars in the School. Instead, the feelings came as a package with the uneven power dynamics and the impression of dependency on the supervisor that most students seem to have (at least at first). That much was obvious to me even then, since rational contextualisation and conceptualisation to parallels with my management experience of the role of power were possible. However, that reflexive awareness accounted for the feelings but did not dissolve them.

So, in sum, I entered a doctoral program with what was too loose a focus, did not consider alternative approaches fully enough, and was probably too dependent on the supervisor's direction. I think my situation was not that unusual, from conversations with others, but an awareness of reflexive practice could have led to a different initial engagement in the research program. Instead, the pivotal change for me came through the interplay of research in the field and grounding in literature. In my non-standard (and non-recommended!) approach, these two activities began in parallel and were iterative.

5.3 GROUNDING IN LITERATURE: 1

Working with literature is a process that can be well aligned with the rational reflexive practices of contextualisation and conceptualisation, and in my case it was very much like that. The steady task of reading, noting and organising material built on and enhanced the contextual frameworks of understanding as masses of material was organised under a number of key concepts. I worked methodically at this task, making a one-page summary of each article (longer for books) in an electronic format, which included my own keywords and any direct quotations that I thought might be helpful. I could see the conceptualis-

ation develop and I updated the keywords on summaries as my enriched scope
for contextualisation grew.

So far, so rational. But given the openness of my initial research topic (what
makes collaboration work?) my initial reading was spread over a vast range
of approaches and themes, to ensure that I had a good handle on (at least)
the headlines of what was already known. Looking back, I could see that the
early establishment of 'defensive boundaries' (as discussed in Chapter 4)
was not very effective. I was able to assimilate a wide range of material, but
I had not paid much attention to the underlying paradigms of the themes I had
integrated. Neither was this breadth offset through the setting of 'offensive
boundaries' (as also discussed in Chapter 4) by focussing on a clear problem,
theme or argument in which paradigm tensions could be addressed through
relational and rational reflexive practices. That would only come later in the
research process (see Grounding in Literature: 2, later in this chapter).

I realised that by jumping into empirical research almost in parallel with
literature engagement, and certainly before I had a clear direction, I was in
a strange dilemma. On the one hand, I could potentially find easier connections to literature if one of the commonly researched themes (say, trust) turned
out to be important in my research contexts, but at the same time there was
more chance of 're-inventing the wheel' when the strategy was so open and
emergent. I could collect data which simply showed past discoveries in a new
setting. On the other hand, if I found a new theme in my field research then
novelty was assured, but connecting to the literature might be more problematic. All of this was contributory to a feeling of mild but steady anxiety about
the future of the research and I could have benefited from more reflexive practice around those emotional perceptions at the time, which could have alerted
me to explore the risks.

There are also traces of a transient increase in emotional temperature,
recorded in my private research notes on some articles, as my engagement with
the literature continued. Extracts from some of these notes are shown verbatim
below, although for the sake of cordial relations with colleagues(!) the article
details are anonymised:

> ...*this model does not appear to have gained widespread acceptance... probably
> because it's bollocks.* [from notes on journal article X]
> *There is a lot more material in this paper that I don't quite grasp, some of which
> may be bullshit.* [from notes on journal article Y]

The arrogance problem I mentioned earlier is clearly evident! In my defence,
I still cited the articles pilloried above, but I was selective about which ideas
I used from them. More importantly, I think the emotional perceptions were
a trigger for more *relational* engagement with the authors through the medium

of their work – I was expecting to receive ideas from them but was having trouble resolving how they fitted with my previous understandings. An angry rejection of possible insights is an easy cop-out in such circumstances. Alternatively, another example note on an article shows how this can lead into rational contextualisation, through eliciting and elaborating the reasons for the emotional reaction, and conceptualising what a more convincing argument would look like:

> *This is all bollocks as far as I am concerned – I strongly agree with the emancipa-*
> *tory project, but I don't think it's necessarily at all reflexive to invoke or suggest*
> *particular RPs in order to support that project – it's just bloody rhetoric. If it was*
> *really reflexive the author would have been at risk/changed her mind in some way...*
> *wouldn't she?* [from notes on journal article Z]

At the time, I generally felt that I was just grumpy! I now think that an emotional perception in a reading experience, that is otherwise anodyne, can be a useful invitation to stop and ask why that reaction happened. That involves treating the text as a conversation partner offering an idea; finding that you can't resolve how the idea could fit with your established experience, you bring forward rational reflexive practice to establish the basis of critique. However, it is also good to check in with your body at the same time – if a quick interoceptive scan shows that after many hours of continuous reading that your neck is stiff, you are hungry and need the bathroom... then maybe you *are* just grumpy.

Overall, I felt that my initial work with literature (intuitively) made good use of rational reflexive practice and of necessity engaged with authors, through their texts, as partners in relational reflexive practice. However, I could have benefited from more deliberate engagement with emotional reflexive practice in two circumstances. First, when perceptions alerted to me to risks inherent in the project at an early stage, there was an opportunity to develop a more focussed approach. That would not have been unusual, since many doctoral students change direction in the early part of their studies. Second, when encountering troublesome ideas in particular sources an emotional reaction is a signal that there may be an important critical take on the literature to be developed, or some particularly tricky concept to grapple with. Later involvement in studies of threshold concepts alerted me to the nature of troublesome knowledge, and the emotional nature of the struggle to assimilate it (Irving, Wright & Hibbert, 2019; Hibbert & Cunliffe, 2015; Wright & Hibbert, 2015). Embodied reflexivity, through an interoceptive scan, would have been useful in knowing how to engage with the critique of some troublesome ideas – or just take a break.

5.4   IDENTIFICATION OF CONTEXTS

Another aspect of my doctoral study that was non-standard was that I began the program as a part-time student, while working as a management consultant. I was lucky in that the company I had joined was focussed on the public sector and involved with multi-sector collaborative organisations supporting science, innovation and industry growth. My employers were supportive of my doctoral study and I was in a position to access multiple contexts that could be appropriate for research focussed on "what makes collaboration work?"

My opportunities largely fitted with both the 'hot' and 'cold' motivations for the selection of contexts. Any context where issues and tensions associated with collaboration were present would have fitted with my personal, hot, emotionally driven interest. Because the literature on collaboration spanned such a wide range of inter-organisational forms, almost all of my consultancy cases, where access could be agreed, would also fit with the research project on a cold, rationally driven (literature informed) basis. Subject to the usual ethical considerations and processes, I actually had too many possibilities to consider, a situation that many researchers would envy. Here is how I described the process of site selection in the early part of my PhD program:

> *The site selection was guided by the opportunities presented [...] Since more opportunities than could be effectively researched were available, the groups studied were selected in accordance with judgements about their likely research interest and relevance.*

That statement does not say much more than 'I went with my gut', really. However, I undertook exploratory research in relatively short-term cases to help me address the dilemmas associated with my loose research framework. This exploratory work was completed early in the process of research (in the first nine months or so) while still developing a literature focus, in order to try to use data and literature *together* to establish a more specific research direction. Looking back, this was a good example of relational reflexive practice in multiple directions, receiving ideas through participant observation and my interpretive engagement with literature, and trying to resolve those different ideas within a common framework that would make sense both in theoretical terms in conversation with the literature, as well as being practically relevant in the field. I was lucky that worked out for me; however, as I discuss later, the final direction of the research was dependent on serendipity to some extent too.

There was, however, some implicit rational reflexive practice in support of generalisability that was evident in the selection of the cases for the main part of the study. I focussed on three different contexts which had some common characteristics – they were cross-sectoral business, technology and science networks. They differed in scale and scope, however, and included a regional, a national (UK) and a European collaborative network. This provided particular opportunities for observing very different groups of individuals within arrangements which had some commonality of purpose.

Another common factor that cannot be overlooked in all of the cases was *me* – I was an active participant with a (different) formal role in each of the networks. Given my goal at that time of supporting generalisability from my work, I argued that my role in each context was relatively minor and was unlikely to 'skew' the ways in which action took place in each context. What was relatively unexplored in that argument was the role of my rational reflexivity, of contextualisation and conceptualisation, in guiding what I *noticed* in each research situation. Given that my focal topic became the role of tradition in the organisation of collaboration (see Hibbert & Huxham, 2010, for example) and that tradition recognises the importance of individual formation (Hibbert, Beech & Siedlok, 2017), this was a pretty big omission. At the time (2001–5) though, I had not developed the ideas about reflexive practice that I now have; in part, that involves awareness of the role of tradition in shaping our own patterns of noticing (Gadamer, 1998) and incorporating that understanding into patterns of engagement with data.

There was also an unexplored opportunity for emotional reflexive practice. While the rationality of my selection of contexts stood up well enough, the selected networks were also situations in which I felt the most comfortable. They all allowed me to present myself on the basis of my original science qualifications and with professional standing as a Chartered Chemist (in comparison with my sense of being 'plankton' in the academic food chain). Moreover, they were situations in which my specific scientific discipline (long since set aside) mattered. In contrast, some other possible contexts – networks focussed on biotechnology, physics or advanced engineering made me feel less at home. I felt less of an 'insider' in those other situations and was often more anxious and less adept in contributing to the progress of projects in those areas. On one hand, perhaps that unfamiliarity would have meant that I had more to learn from my research, if I had addressed the emotional perceptions more directly? On the other hand, every doctoral study involves choices and there is never enough time to do all that we want, so perhaps the emotional perceptions allowed me to avoid getting bogged down in situations where the research process would have offered more difficulty than I could process. Looking back, I think that the latter was more likely to have been the case, but that view is seen through the lens of a doctoral research project that worked well enough and was completed successfully.

Despite some missed opportunities for early reflexive practice (an omission which, pragmatically, made it easier to collect a diverse range of material quickly) the range of geographical and organisational contexts that I selected *did* help to support arguments about the generalisability of the findings. Favouring longer term and higher frequency of contact opportunities (multiple engagements with each network over extended time frames – between 1 and 3 years) was also helpful in convincing others, especially during the process of publishing papers from the research, about the robustness of the insights (and I will come back to the challenges of publication later in the chapter).

Overall, I think that the process for identifying contexts for research that I used was mostly cold, with hidden hot spots here and there, although I certainly did not pay enough attention to the emotional perceptions in the early part of my research. I wonder if that is partly the reason why it has become something of a recurring theme in my research in recent times, since completing the doctoral program all those years ago, to pay more attention to the problems and potential of emotions in supporting learning and adaptation? In any case, I think that the missed opportunities for reflexive practice, in relation to my identification of research contexts, could also resonate with others. I speculate that better engagement with reflexive practice in this part of the research process could be helpful for most researchers undertaking interpretive research, especially if they are lucky enough to have multiple choices of location.

5.5   GROUNDING IN LITERATURE: 2

The normal expectation of engagement with literature in a doctoral research project is that of a 'funnel pattern' – ideas from broad reading are integrated, and a narrower focus is developed. Eventually a gap is spotted, in the form of some small corner of the field that is missing a key insight. That missing link becomes the focus of the research question, which we then build our research around. Other approaches take a similar line, but take a view based on the suspicion that the field is burgeoning (many new concepts are still emerging) and so there is potential to add to them through focussing on a relatively broad, open and exploratory research question that spots new concept(s) in data rather than literature. An alternative approach to either of these strategies is to problematise, by looking at a well-researched phenomenon or situation from a completely different theoretical perspective (for different perspectives on problematisation see Locke & Golden-Biddle, 1997 and Sandberg & Alvesson, 2011). My approach, engaging in research in the field before settling on a precise research question was aligned with the second approach, based on the suspicion that more can be understood about a particular theme than has been conceptualised in the extant literature.

The reason that the second approach can be a reasonable risk to take is because of the broad range of ideas that are carried into understanding in the early stages of reading, which may open up a wide range of adjacent themes

based on our own experience. The rational reflexive practice of contextualisation has a lot of material to work with. For example, the range of concepts
addressed in early stage reading on collaboration during my doctoral research
included: different bases for theorising about collaboration, as varied as institutional theory, network theories, discourse approaches and transaction cost
economics; key factors in the successful organisation of collaboration, such as
trust, power, culture, communication, leadership and structural arrangements;
and different ways of recognising success. (See Cropper, Ebers, Huxham &
Ring, 2008, for an overview of such themes.) If I had remained within this
admittedly wide set of established themes, I would probably have focussed
on culture. There had not been a great deal written on culture in collaboration
at the time (and even less focussed on culture in cross-sectoral business,
technology and science networks) and I was gathering observations which
showed that this could be an important theme. However, I ended up following
a different path, not because of reading within the field, but because of reading
outside of the field.

I had a chance encounter with the ideas of hermeneutics through an overly
wide and early search for interpretive methodology resources. That broad
search came about because I was entering the field to conduct research while
still developing my literature framework. Reading into and around interpretiv-
ism led me, via a couple of twists and turns, to Gadamer's (1960/1998) *Truth
and Method*, focussed on philosophical hermeneutics. Amongst other things,
the book made me aware of the role of tradition in shaping interpretation and
our patterns of understanding. That lead me to Shils' (1981) masterwork on
tradition and I was hooked.

To illuminate this choice and perhaps seek to share some of my enthusiasm,
I think it is helpful to mention in brief what my focus on tradition entailed.
The simplest conceptualisation of tradition is that it is something transmitted
– handed down or handed on – as well as the description of this process of
transmission:

> *Constellations of symbols, clusters of images, are received and modified. They
> change in the process of transmission as interpretations are made of the tradition
> presented; they change also while they are in the possession of their recipients. This
> chain of transmitted variants is also called a tradition...* (Shils, 1981, p. 13)

The process of transmission of tradition generates an authoritative pattern of
interpretation, which does not close down all alternative meanings but instead
favours certain possibilities over others, without nailing down every detail:

> *...This is in fact always the case when something speaks to us from tradition: there
> is something evident about what is said, though that does not imply it is, in every*

> *detail, secured, judged and decided. The tradition asserts its own truth in being understood...* (Gadamer, 1998, p. 486)

Following Shils' characterisation and building on Gadamer's philosophy, the theory of tradition diverted me towards a problematising approach. It offered a possible explanation for how cultures develop and endure that had not been applied in my field, as well as providing a more parsimonious explanation for social structures and their effects on individuals than other approaches (see Hibbert & Huxham, 2010, 2011). It seems strange looking back, but I was *really excited* by the prospect of engaging with the theory of tradition! This was another time when emotional reflexive practice could have alerted me to the fact that I should stop and examine what was going on.

While tradition turned out to be an interesting and productive focus for the main tranche of my research, I had not considered the problems that might arise from studying it. The first issue was related to my problems with reflexive contextualisation. Shils' (1981) theory of tradition is worked out in considerable detail and supports a view of it having a pivotal role in society affecting social structures, culture, community and individual identity, as well as what counts as knowledge. All of those themes have complex literatures which I too found it difficult to disentangle. I will discuss the difficulty of dealing with these entanglements in more detail later, in the section covering analysis. The second issue was the similar problems of reflexive contextualisation applied by *others* when I was presenting ideas about the role of tradition; as an unfamiliar theory, others tended to grasp it within their own frames of reference and file it under more popular and 'similar feeling' themes, such as culture or institutional theory. I will also elaborate on the resulting problems associated with responding to critique later in this chapter. For the present, having explained how I had settled on a more precise research focus for the study, I will discuss reflexive practice in the context of data collection.

5.6   CHOICES ABOUT DATA COLLECTION

An interesting aspect of my PhD research trajectory, mentioned above, is that the contexts for research were established before the research question was really refined. As mentioned earlier, a problem that I encountered was that a potentially overwhelming volume of data could be available (when the initial research question was so broad), which would be a struggle to capture and collate. However, once the second stage of literature engagement had helped to sharpen the focus, that problem was reduced by selecting a subset of sites for data collection and using theory as a loose guide for shaping data collection. What I mean by that is that the focus on tradition helped to bring certain things into view more sharply (while obscuring some others).

Practically, data were primarily collected through participant observation during collaborative meetings and processes within each of the three focal networks that formed the contexts for the research. Much of the material was in the form of notes taken during events or written up immediately after they had taken place. 'Offline' discussions with participants away from collaborative locations also provided additional material related to observational data and often included unstructured discussions focussed upon the operation and success of the particular network. Where offline discussions took place face-to-face, they were noted 'naturally' as part of an attentive engagement. Where this was not possible, notes were recorded immediately after the conversation. Telephone discussions were noted at the time of the call, as closely as possible, where this was practicable. In addition, all collaborative outputs (co-developed network process models, formal reports and so on) and textual transactions (memos, emails, contributory reports and other written materials) were retained to provide a range of different types of data for each case.

What is lost, within that standard account of the technicalities of data collection, are the reflexive practices that enhanced or obstructed a focus on particular data items or sources. Although not always recognised at the time, there were a lot of influences and insights in play that could have been engaged with more carefully, through better attention to reflexive practice. For example, at one point I came to realise that my notes included a lot of material related to one particular participant in one of the networks. It took me a while to realise that this focus was *not* related to the importance of his contribution to the development of the network or the deep insights into the role of tradition that engaging with him afforded. Instead, my focus was drawn because he was handsome and witty! Such issues are ethical conflicts as well as reflexive practice challenges, of course. But there is a need to remember our humanity in field research and that our emotional perceptions may be engaged, as well as noting interoceptive insights. If a research participant makes your heart beat faster, what should you do...? I would like to be able to write, at this point: 'reader, I married him'... but instead I made an effort to engage more widely with others in the network instead, in order to correct the imbalance of my attention. What a fool.

It was interesting to note, looking back, that negative emotional perceptions about others did *not* have the opposite effect to positive perceptions. Feelings of anger or sadness in relation to particular participants, for example, made their actions more memorable whether I felt a personal connection to them or not. These feelings probably had more of a role than I realised, at the time, in noticing material for data collection when it related to things that individuals said or wrote, or their actions (or inactions, when divergent from the norm). It is likely that these trigger points for looking into a context more deeply will have shaped the data collection in amplified ways, through holding my attention to certain aspects of the context at the expense of others. To some degree the effects of emotional engagement could also have led, through that process of amplification, to decisions about how long to remain in the field for particular cases. Did I look a little less deeply in contexts involving emotionally neutral situations in comparison to those where emotional perceptions were evident, so that a feeling of saturation arrived sooner in unemotive contexts? Probably.

In addition to the effects of emotional and embodied reflexivity (of which I was not always fully aware), there were also missed opportunities for enriching the meaningfulness of data collection that rational reflexive practice could have improved. In particular, while I am sure that I was also using my everyday abilities for interpretation through apperception as I gathered data, rather than just being led by emotional perceptions, the pressure of time and attention meant that I noted the material in a way that short-cut some of the potential insights. What I mean here is that I would rapidly note material in ways that conceptualised as well as recorded it (it is impossible to avoid this unless using recording technology, and even then, noticing certain material as interesting within a recording may just be a delayed version of the same rapid engagement), but did not explicate (what I could) about the contextualisation. In this way, there were a lot of missed insights about *why* I was noticing particular material as worthy of observational notes. That kind of rationally reflexive practice could have helped me to spot opportunities for connecting and building themes sooner, as well as potentially alerting me to 'blind spots' in my data collection (what was missing or overplayed in my contextualisation), in much the same way that nascent emotional reflexive practice did, in time.

Looking back, it is clear that the importance of relational reflexive practice – which leads to engaging with participants in rich ways, that reveal something of their hinterland as well as the ideas we receive from them in a given moment – was not something that I deliberately or intuitively applied during my PhD research with any clarity. I did develop relational connections with participants over time, which helped unfocussed understandings to be resolved, but at the time (building, perhaps on some specific emotional boundary issues touched on earlier) I perceived relationships to be a complicating ethical issue in the main (for more on this, see Beech, Hibbert, McInnes & MacIntosh, 2009). This is *the* great loss from trying to support a research process tilted strongly towards generalisation. Interpretive research in the field does not – should not – have to be defended on criteria that would be appropriate for methods that seek to be objective. I might have had more interesting results if I had accepted the subjectivity and intersubjectivity of the process and focussed more on relationships, tilting towards closeness rather than distanciation from others with whom I was working in the contexts of my research. However, these are difficult choices when you are a PhD student, whose future career prospects depend on achieving the doctorate and developing publishable articles from the material. Those possibilities depend on both the data that are collected and how it is analysed to generate shareable insights.

5.7   APPROACHES TO ANALYSIS AND GENERATING SHAREABLE INSIGHTS

I had decided to treat each of the three research contexts separately, on the basis that evidence of themes or concepts that were common to multiple and quite different settings would give strong support for generalisability. That decision had really been 'baked in' with the selection of contexts earlier in the study, of course. In working with the data for each case, my analytical engagement sought to follow the principles for supporting the development of 'emergent theory' outlined by Eden and Huxham (1996) and elaborated later in my work with Chris Huxham (Huxham & Hibbert, 2011). In the following, I set out what that process involved, while adding in post-hoc thoughts about how reflexive practice was involved or overlooked as a missed opportunity.

I worked through the empirical material collected for each of the three study contexts in turn, beginning with the smallest (I was involved in the three contexts for periods of roughly one year, two years and three years, and the volume of material for each context reflected that). This was a deliberate rational reflexive choice, allowing for some sensitisation to emergent themes to speed up engagement with the larger cases while allowing space for new concepts to be discerned from increasingly larger bodies of material. Although I would not have used the terms at the time, I was aware that my developing capacity for the rationally reflexive contextualisation of the data would potentially shut down the possibility of noticing alternatives in the smaller cases, if a range of plausible-enough major themes had been developed for the larger cases. Of course, it was also less daunting to start with the shortest case!

For each case, the material was reviewed and simple abstracts, which might be viewed as 'entry points' to the more richly situated descriptions of / connections in the data in the full records, were identified. The selection criteria for the abstracts were loosely applied guides: generalised statements about how theories of tradition might be evident in the material, that were characterised through the development of a preliminary conceptual model used to integrate the literature. Specifically, I examined the data for evidence of:

- The continuity of practices, reasoning or values from the past, especially despite changing circumstances (the continuity provided by tradition, a key aspect of the literature).
- Conflicts or difficulties associated with (perceptions of) identity – and differences amongst identities (based on the arguments about the traditional and cultural constitution of identity).

- Traces of the authority of tradition in the apparent ways in which partic∙ipants construed events (connected to the traditional/cultural construction of knowledge).
- Implicit structural power relations, for example shown in unchallenged instances of 'domination' (connected to the role of tradition's authoritative support for establishing structures and maintaining them).

If you find it to be of specific interest, more on the underlying themes involved in understanding tradition and how these play out in the development of theory is discussed in the main publications from my thesis (Hibbert & Huxham, 2010, 2011).

However, the main point for the present argument is that using very broad statements provided a way of capturing a wide range of excerpts from the data as a starting point for engagement. As the excerpts were selected, emerging categories could be developed from them which formed new 'selection criteria' allowing broader patterns to be incorporated, some of which suggested additional ideas to consider. To understand how this works, imagine sorting a stack of cards which includes hundreds of individual pictures and a standard deck of playing cards. You might select the playing cards, and then realise you can sort based on main colour and repeated shapes – you should end up with two or four ways of arranging them in sets. But as you are sorting those non-blank cards you notice other categories – the use of letters or numbers, the presence or absence of figurative pictures, military symbols and gender representations, which add further criteria. You might then return to the other cards looking for material based on those themes. The end result is a rich view of the whole data set, beginning with simple sorting concepts evident from theory but open to other categories that become apparent in the 'sorting' process.

In the case of my empirical material, the excerpts selected and sorted in this way were utterances – either in context settings or during telephone conversations, physical actions (choices of seating, movement and so on) and inactions (noted lack of engagement during collaborative processes, unexplained or explained absences, and so on) and parts of written communications and formal documents. The excerpts were concise points – usually no more than around twenty words – which were transferred to a 'conceptual mapping' software application, clustered and linked to produce visual 'maps' of the data that were described in narrative form. For more on this approach to inductive interpretive analysis, see Huxham and Hibbert (2010) and the resultant themes developed in Hibbert and Huxham (2010) and Huxham and Hibbert (2011). Overall, this was a useful approach for interpreting data through a particular theory lens and provided a good way of seeing multiple possibilities in the data. But it came with some reflexive and practical problems too.

The *reflexive problem*, that is masked by a neutral account of the analysis, is the illusion that interpretation is deferred to the analytical stage of the research. As mentioned earlier, observational data are always already interpreted in the act of noticing some things and not others, and in the words that you choose to describe what you see. I didn't realise quite how much the latter point was true for me until I was questioned on the 'ironic tone' of many of my observations during my PhD *viva voce* examination! So, the missing aspect of reflexive practice in my data collection – noting what is going on in the contextualis-ation, in other words *why* I noticed – and how that influences conceptualisation was important. This means that if you have not built the practice in, there is a need to be able to look back on these matters through relatively crude processes of introspection, in order to audit the analysis for your influence on both the data notices and collected and your 'feeling' for their significance. For example, I noted in the final version of my thesis that:

- I was raised in a poor family, and this may lead to a particular sensitivity to extravagant displays of wealth and/or power (a theme of privilege and establishment influence was prominent in my analysis of tradition in one of the study contexts).
- As a gay man, issues related to (especially stereotypical or power-related) gender roles may be something that I am particularly sensitised to (again, this was a prominent theme in some of the cases considered in my study).

It would have been much more interesting and constructive to delve behind these crude statements with a more fine-grained approach during data collec-tion rather than during analysis, which could have led me to collect additional insightful data.

The *practical problem* was related to producing shareable insights, in two ways. First, the conceptual maps were produced using a specific software tool and a methodological approach favoured by only my doctoral supervisor and (literally) a handful of others. It meant that any (visual) representation of the data was less likely to be understood or appreciated by readers than many more common and familiar ways of tabulating qualitative data. Second, the combination of my observational approach combined with a complex interpretive analysis made it difficult (compared to, say, sharing tabulated interview data) to 'show' readers the source of insights rather than 'tell' them. This is a missing and deferred aspect of facilitating *others'* relational reflexive practice that I could have worked harder on during the doctoral study. Finding ways to present data so that those with other perspectives could more easily receive the ideas, as well as allowing the process of resolving our understand-ing be more straightforward, would have eased my path to publication later.

Part of that publication challenge is also addressed, of course, through writing in ways that connect findings into the literature conversation.

5.8   RECONNECTING TO LITERATURE AND READERS: WRITING INTO A CONVERSATION

I found the experience of writing-up a doctoral thesis to be something like a strange and dispiriting sort of conversation. The exchange was mostly with myself, since earlier engagement with others through literature had largely been completed. I was mainly working with ideas that I had already assimilated from those others, which now formed part of my own frameworks for the reflexive practice of contextualisation. This meant that conceptualisations that tied together insights from the data with literature connections were generated without the need to return to the literature and re-read (other than the usual check for the latest publications in the field). This conversation with myself was dispiriting because, once I had developed the writing sufficiently to complete my own understanding, I was completely bored by the need to re-write in order to make the insights clear to others. Nevertheless, without realising it, I was on a trajectory to re-joining a theoretical conversation on my own terms.

However, the relational reflexive engagement necessary to re-join the conversation was underplayed, with effects on style as well as content. Overall, I found that I was trying to write my work to show it had achieved doctoral standard and for my own comfort (and these are not unnatural motivations at the end of a PhD), rather than writing with others in mind. I think this is a problem not just for me, but reflects researcher training in general. The scientific model of the thesis leads us to 'write up our results' in a defensive, neutral way, rather than thinking about how we might engage the reader, at a distance, in an intellectual conversation. This is not a huge problem in relation to 'getting the thesis over the line', but it does cause knock-on problems when adapting the work for publication.

Thus, even though I sought to develop a narrative form for my findings, I was still doing that in a mechanical way rather than thinking carefully (informed by an expectation of relational reflexive practice) about style and engagement. In addition, I had not looked deeply enough at how to move from narrative findings to a more thematic argument in a formal discussion section, or whether that was the right way to go about connecting findings back to the literature for every kind of research. That is not to say that my style was sci-entific or *completely* neutral. Instead, my intention to support a shared under-standing was over-weighted towards my unconsidered writing preferences (the ironic style noted by an examiner, for example) and missed the need to set up cues about authenticity, plausibility and criticality that could have shaped and guided other readers' engagement (Golden-Biddle & Locke, 1993, 1997).

Establishing those cues may have aligned the reader, as they transitioned from findings to discussion, to be already 'set up' to receive the connections in a certain way. Those rhetorical cues could have been explored and developed through more relationally reflexive attention to *how* the extant literature was written, as well as *what* it presented. That is, 'asking' published articles about their way of speaking as well as their message. This was a missed opportunity in the preparation of the thesis, that had to be addressed in extensive re-writing for later publications. However, as everyone eventually discovers, every journal has a style that evolves over time, so this is always a moving target.

There were other missed opportunities too. For me, and I suspect for many, the writing phase was very intense and coupled with anxiety about the examination that would follow, as well as distracting concerns about the need to find my first lecturing post at the same time. Emotional reflexive practice around this time would have made me more aware of these perceptions of anxiety and helped me to consider how they impacted on the flow of writing. The longer the writing process continued, the more defensive I became about the text that I regarded as finished. I became increasingly reticent in relation to (even sensible) changes that were recommended, as the thesis submission date drew closer. I also omitted some complex materials – convoluted data diagrams – which I thought were not centrally necessary, on the basis that they might lead to a challenging conversation in the *viva voce* examination (as mentioned earlier, I was using a non-standard method that would be unfamiliar to most). Of course, this just led to an even more complicated conversation in the examination since it left a gap in the presentation of the material.

Looking back, better attention to emotional reflexive practice might have helped me to realise that I was allowing my perceptions of anxiety and fear to dominate my choices; combining this with interoceptive attention to the tenseness in my body would have confirmed that too. This is not to say that those emotions were wrong or entirely unhelpful. At times the stress was at the motivational level, driving me to push on with the writing. But there was a definite need for balance that was missed. It was actually really helpful to be able to (re)write over 4000 words a day at times, but that hectic pace comes with the corollary that what is written will need a lot of refinement before it is ready for external critique.

5.9   RESPONDING TO CRITIQUE

In Chapter 4, I emphasised the positive aspects of external critique in the process of developing research for publication. The main benefit, from a reflexive perspective, is the opportunity for employing the relational reflexive practices of reception and resolution on both 'sides' of the conversation between authors and peer reviewers. Of course, while it is helpful to frame the exchange in that way, not all peer reviewers see it in the same light. Some seem to take a more combative approach, looking over work for flaws that need to be eliminated based on the lack of fit with their own rationally reflexive contextualisation of the field (without necessarily conceiving it in those terms). Thus, while journal editors (including me) like to see the review process as a collaborative conversation, it is not always so. Like everyone else, I learned how to respond to (comments I interpreted as) barbed criticism with polite thankfulness (and other forms of disingenuousness) in the response letters that accompany revised papers back into the bearpit. You will have noticed that my emotions, associated with writing struggles, have not gone away...

Partly because of the vagaries of responding to reviewers, the emotional perceptions during the submission and revision processes were more significant than I had expected. They were also of longer duration. In addition to some collaborative contributions to edited books, the main publications from my PhD research took the form of two journal articles and it was a long time before they reached final publication – around four years in each case. During that time, I worked on other projects in parallel and learned to adapt. I found that the approach of reading the journal's decision letter and reviewer recommendations in two stages, as recommended by a friend, to be helpful. The first reading is a quick one, to take the emotional 'hit' of the review comments about the writing we have invested so much in. The second reading – at least a week later – is dedicated to the relationally reflexive turn, in which we try to receive and resolve the thoughts the reviewers offer. Here is where I make an important balancing observation, to offset my remarks about the negative approach of some reviewers: I am sure that every publication I have ever produced was improved by at least *some* of the reviewers' observations.

I also mentioned, in Chapter 4, the aim of staying true to our motivations in thinking about where our research is published. However, in practice I found that I had so much invested in trying to fit with a particular journal that wrenching it out mid-process would have been an alarming prospect, even when I felt that I was compromising what I wished to add to debates. However, that does reflect the fact that my PhD research was at least seeking to take an observational (if not objective) stance with little trace of my presence in the field in the text. Since the writing was not about me *personally* that made the compromises seem easier (even though research processes usually involve personal identity work to some extent: see Callagher, El Sahn, Hibbert, Korber & Siedlok, 2021). In addition, it is important to note that the publication process includes some compromises that are not easily expressed in relational reflexive practice terms. Publication is a power game as well as an intellectual one, and newly minted PhDs do not have a lot of power.

Overall, I think I could have done more to develop emotional reflexive practice in connection with rational reflexive practice, to have a clearer sense of what felt important to me in the writing (for example, when I experienced an emotional reaction in response to my writing being challenged) and to go on from that to work out why, through examining how it was contextualised in my experience. What other experiences or insights was it connected to, and how did the whole pattern matter or not? With that more clearly in view, perhaps the years-long processes of submitting and revision, along the way to publication in journals, might have been easier to handle.

5.10 OVERVIEW

Compared to the 'ideal type' or theoretical perspective set out in Chapter 4, some different patterns of reflexive practices played out in my doctoral research in each of the phases. Importantly, there were three factors underpinning many of the differences. The first factor was my simple lack of a fully developed awareness and habit of reflexive practice. My descriptions here have involved interpreting a less fully formed and perhaps even nascent approach, using the set of terms outlined earlier, and it is no surprise that the pattern looks less than ideal. Second, the rather neutral account set out in the earlier chapter does not consider the precarious and anxious situation of the average PhD student, which leaves a lot of emotional perceptions to be addressed (or ignored) whether they advance the research process or not. My experience of the anxiety inherent in steps of the doctoral journey was consistent with that of most of my colleagues. The final factor is related to the second, namely the power and relationship dynamics which are not easily handled by research-focussed reflexive practices – for example situations where research participants come to be friends, or senior figures in the disciplinary field exert their influence. In addition to the three factors, a more detailed summary of variations and opportunities for reflexive practice across the phases is provided in Table 5.1.

Table 5.1   *Variations in (implicit) reflexive practice during doctoral research*

Element of the research process	Problems, opportunities and variations in reflexive practice in the doctoral research case study
Characterisation and commitment	An initial over-reliance on relational reflexive (reception and resolution) practices and dependency on the supervisor, and less scope for rational reflexive practice (especially in relation to contextualisation). The initial motivation was very *hot*; although that was quickly superseded, the lack of emotional and embodied reflexive practices (perception and interoception) meant that the influence of the emotional motivation was not accounted for and challenged at the time.
Grounding in literature	The theoretical picture suggests that this is a balance of rational reflexive practices and relational reflexive practices, with authors engaged as intellectual conversation partners through their texts. But the emotional perception of 'troublesome' ideas and the embodied nature of (extended) reading also influenced how literature was (and is) assimilated.
Identification of contexts	The selection of contexts was partly opportunistic. While the research sites were still a rational (reflexive) fit with the literature framing and intended direction of the research, choices were also influenced by an emotional perception of 'fitting in' within some contexts and feeling less at home in others. Using such emotional perceptions as an invitation to follow up with rational reflexive practice could have helped to establish how experience was mobilised to locate and shape the research (and the assumptions that went along with that).
Choices about data collection	Rational reflexive practice was the clear driver for decisions about what kinds of data to collect and for how long. Relational reflexive practice was relatively unfamiliar at the time, and was not mobilised. Emotional and embodied reflexive practices slowly came into awareness, in the recognition that research contexts are places where people interact in their full humanity.
Approaches to analysis and generating shareable insights	The doctoral experience confirmed that engagement with rational and relational reflexive practice are both necessary, in finding ways to share the full range of insights in conceptualisations that can be understood (well enough) by others and have some utility for them. However, the experience also showed that interpretive analysis begins in the 'noticing' of data and how it is recorded, so finding ways to interrogate what is going on in that contextualisation and conceptualisation, *during data collection*, would be helpful.

Element of the research process	Problems, opportunities and variations in reflexive practice in the doctoral research case study
Reconnecting to literature and readers: writing into a conversation	Rational and relational reflexive practice were relevant to establish a (hope for) connection with readers, but the need to focus on style as well as content as a basis for connection was missed. Initial writing, in the context of an impending examination, was also negatively shaped by emotional perceptions of fear and anxiety, which led to some unhelpful defensive choices.
Responding to critique	Emotional and embodied reflexive practice were not necessarily triggered by critique that pushed against the limits of authenticity, but instead by the general level of anxiety and uncertainty. Emotions normally needed to be given space first before rational and relational reflexive practice could be engaged in order to respond productively to critique. Paying attention to emotional perceptions and interpreting those feelings from another level could have helped to show what was going on, in relation to reactions to the kinds of critical comments that are intrinsic to review processes.

While the general factors underpinning differences may apply to any doctoral project, the likely pattern in each will be as different as each individual researcher. Nevertheless, there are some additional general conclusions that may be useful for those contemplating or guiding doctoral research. As with the ideal type in the earlier Table (4.1), in this case certain reflexive practices were foregrounded in particular phases of the research, while the other types of reflexive practice were potentially active at the same time but receiving less attention. My conclusion is that my doctoral research shows that reflexive practices do not need to be named according to my (or any other) scheme in order to go on, but having a way to recognise and name the practices does help us to be aware of them even long after the fact. So, if the need to demonstrate or be aware of reflexivity occurs after the events have passed, it is likely that someone can give an account of it – to some degree – retrospectively, even if the benefits of a more informed and aware engagement have slipped away.

As mentioned in Chapter 4, some form of research diary is a useful way to capture insights about what might otherwise be harder to recover and the advice about what to note in it – the full spectrum of embodied, emotional, rational and relational insights that come to awareness – applies too. To that advice, I would like to add a further suggestion. It is helpful, from time-to-time, to deliberately question what is going on in another reflexive level from the one that is currently in the foreground. For example, if you are a doctoral student and your diary notes unchallenged reception of ideas from your supervisor, (what) did you think about it? Have those ideas been assimilated through apperception or simply received as blunt fact, whether they fit with your earlier understanding or not? Or, as another example, if you are strongly drawn to something happening in the field which seems especially interesting

– or conversely, unbearable to watch – have you asked yourself how you are feeling and whether your emotional and/or bodily state is disturbed? Of course, we would be immobilised by attending to these questions all the time, but a 'check-in' with yourself from time-to-time is helpful, especially when you are making significant decisions about the direction of the research or believe you have discovered something pivotal.

Dialogue

1. In a relatively limited space, I have tried to give an overview of both how it *felt* to complete a PhD and identify opportunities for reflexive practice in relation to that. What would you like to have learned more about, and where might you find that?
2. I have very briefly suggested that there are some issues – like power – which are not easily *managed* through reflexive practice. Do you agree? What else is difficult to manage through reflexive practice?
3. I have recommended the use of a research diary and employing reflexive practices from alternative levels in order to capture insights. How do these approaches fit into your approach to doctoral study, or compare with your advice for students?

NOTES

1. Different systems use different terms for the same role; hereafter I use the term 'supervisor' for conciseness, since that was the term used during my time at my doctoral institution.
2. There are doctoral programs that take a different approach, particularly (but not only) professional doctorates where the focus is on generating an *applied* contribution to knowledge.

6. Case study: reflexive practice in collaborative research

I was working with my friends in their office in the University of Auckland. We had finished writing the final draft of our paper together, after which I had just completed the formatting checks in order to send it to a journal. Another friend (not involved with the project) dropped in, and I proudly mentioned we had our paper ready to go. She looked at my screen, where the abstract of the paper was visible, and commented:
"That sounds bland – it doesn't tell me anything specific about what you have learned. Do you think you should say more about the actual contribution?"
*I felt quite frustrated at that moment, since the relief of having something completed was taken away and even worse, she was absolutely right – it **was** bland and non-specific.*

6.1 THE EXTENDED PROCESS OF COLLABORATIVE, REFLEXIVE RESEARCH

It seems to be a feature of collaborative research that it approaches completion only for another round of work to follow. This sense of stretching and re-starting is amplified when engaged in relational reflexive practice, since there is an intention to receive new ideas from others and try to resolve their impact on the study – even if they are just someone taking a casual glance, there is still a need to at least entertain their suggestions. Despite the occasional frustrating moment, this is actually a positive benefit for projects where the intention is to make a connection with readers. That intention involves (as discussed in Chapter 2) to make the work meaningful by seeking to:

Maximise the authenticity and resonance of the understandings generated in their research projects, through drawing attention to and building on the richness of their situated interpretive stance, as much as that is possible.

The more views and insights on the work that are generated, the more opportunity there is to evaluate whether other readers may be likely to see something meaningful in it, that resonates with them.

The focus of this chapter was such a project, intended to maximise authenticity and resonance. It involved a collaborative group – working together as part of a wider program of research – of which I was one member. Our focus on this occasion was to research how we learn and adapt in response to challenging, negative emotional experiences. The group changed shape for different projects but for the focal example in this chapter it involved four people: I worked with Nic Beech (based in the UK) and Lisa Callagher and Frank Siedlok (based in New Zealand). Although the completion of the writing and publication processes took place at the time of the COVID-19 pandemic, we were able to work around the difficulties. This was possible because we *had* been able to meet in earlier stages and most of our later collaboration was online. The principal output from the project was a journal article, but it also led to further ideas that we were still exploring at the time this book was written.

The project was the third time that I had worked with collaborators using a specific relationally reflexive approach (Hibbert, Sillince, Diefenbach & Cunliffe, 2014), applied in an autoethnographic mode, in which the researchers took a dual role as participants providing our own experiences as the material for the study. This approach means that the researchers are also fully present in the study as unmediated participants, which enables them to be able to 'speak authentically'. Ideally, the resonance of the understandings generated through the approach is supported through relational reflexive practices of receiving and resolving, involving a specific focus on engaging with others and enacting connections with them across the research process.

We began to work on the study (along with other projects) in 2017 and it was eventually accepted for publication in 2021. This timescale may seem to be protracted, but it is important to note that a relationally reflexive, autoethnographic research approach would be considered by many to be more risky and less mainstream; indeed, the first paper using this approach from the wider program (Hibbert, Callagher, Siedlok, Windahl & Kim, 2019) was published in a journal which specifically seeks to accommodate non-traditional research. However, the publication timescale was *not* actually lengthier than the norm for more traditional forms of research in my field, although the range of possible outlets for publication was more limited than it might be for more conventional work.

Having established the purpose and context, the rest of the chapter proceeds in this way. I step through each of the phases discussed in Chapter 4, explaining how reflexive practice was involved in that phase as it was experienced in this research project. In doing so, I highlight how this process varies from the 'ideal type'. You will immediately notice that the order of the phases or activities is different, but I also draw out some more detailed nuances. I then summarise the patterns of reflexive practice and the problems that needed to be addressed, after which I explore how we might continue to support and develop this approach.

6.2 CHARACTERISATION, MOTIVATIONS AND COMMITMENT

Collaborative research with a focus on authenticity and resonance is not likely to have an initial cold, literature-derived motivation. Participant researchers will need to feel that the focus of the study is an area where they have relevant personal experience, along with a sense that the *possible* theme is not something that they have already encountered in their scholarly reading. For Nic, Lisa, Frank and I our motivation came from discussing incidents in our careers where negative emotions had "derailed" us, at least temporarily. We realised that these incidents had some common features: we felt the unresolved pain of the events long after the incidents, in some cases many years after. We wanted to understand the processes that led to us holding on to these painful experiences, and we wanted to know how we might deal with those kinds of experiences in the future.

This kind of engagement with a shared issue was not planned. The engagement emerged, instead, from the shared practice of relational reflexivity. This was partly because we had developed trusting relationships, in which the practice of receiving ideas from others and discussing them was normal. We were aware of differences in our life experiences and expected that others would have insights, and interpretations of themes of interest, that would differ from and add to our own. The practice of resolving these interpretations, at the outset of the study, was really about enacting connections with the otherness that we had engaged (Hibbert, Sillince, Diefenbach & Cunliffe, 2014). A simpler way of putting that is to say that we engaged with each other's interpretations of experience, enough to ensure that we had the basis of a shared conversation that could support a commitment to the research study at the heart of this case.

It is important to emphasise that this generation of a shared interest through conversation was not instrumental. The process was only possible because we enjoyed working together as a group: our conversations and time together were (and still are) important socially as well as professionally. This was both a benefit and a risk for the progress of the study. On the positive side, social connections helped to keep the group together for the long haul of the research process. On the negative side, if the research did not go well, or intellectual differences developed, then it could have felt that there was much more at stake than "just a research paper". However, I do not think there is a choice about whether to commit to research in which we are *personally* engaged, by which I mean when the research theme matters to us as individuals, especially when taking an autoethnographic approach and sharing life experiences with collaborators. In any case, relational reflexive practice is intrinsic to the social processes, practices and relationships that occur between us whether we are researchers, participants or simply persons (Hibbert, Sillince, Diefenbach & Cunliffe, 2014; Lambrechts, Grieten, Bouwen & Corthouts, 2009; Steyaert & Van Looy, 2010). A foundational social dimension seems to be unavoidable for relationally reflexive collaboration and on balance it is helpful when that social dimension is imbued with friendship. I suggest that this kind of personal engagement with others presents another kind of motivation for engaging in the research project: rather than 'hot' or 'cold', it is 'warm', in the caring sense.

Warm motivations and caring sentiments can lead to strong commitments. This has been evident in projects with friends that I have been involved with, when some research themes have sprung into life unexpectedly, during purely social conversation. For example, one of my colleagues suggested that a really authentic opening line for the methodology section of a collaborative paper on discrimination and identity work (Callagher, El Sahn, Hibbert, Korber & Siedlok, 2021) would read: "...we were having coffee and cake in a really nice French patisserie when someone mentioned..." He was right, of course, but I lacked the courage for sharing that level of detail. However, it serves to underline that this kind of approach benefits greatly from two kinds of openness that are involved with warm motivations. One kind of openness is the willingness to embrace serendipity – being ready to engage with something unexpected and to recognise that something interesting might be going on that is worth exploring – just as you would in any friendly conversation.

The second kind of openness is towards seeing serendipitous insights as an invitation to reflexive practice, motivated by care for the person who offers the insight. Taking advantage of that invitation worked for us as a group of friends because we had developed a habit of reflexive practice alongside our social relationship. When "someone mentioned..." it spurred a different level of conversation because it was a surprising (or perhaps shocking) incident that was discussed. Here is the incident in question, that launched an earlier study: a business owner, interviewed for a conventional study, had asked a researcher who was an immigrant "what boat did you get off?". Relational reflexive practice helped the rest of us receive the new insight and quickly resolve our interpretation of it as an instance of discrimination. However, our individual rational reflexive practices offered a range of contextualisation and conceptualisation possibilities, when we tried to understand how experiences like that had impacted on us and our careers in different ways. It was a need to understand *that* issue – the effect of discrimination on our careers – that became the focus, because we cared about the effects these incidents had on each other. That motivated us to engage in that earlier research study.

The same pattern of motivation was true of the project that is the main focus of this case study chapter. We understood each other in relation to how we characterised the central concept of negative emotional experiences, but we had a range of interpretations about the effects of those experiences on our own and others' lives. We felt that developing a better understanding of the dynamics behind these effects, in a shareable narrative, would allow us to help each other and could resonate with those beyond our group, in ways that would be interesting and useful.

Our shared commitment to this study on negative emotional experiences was reached without any formal engagement with literature at the outset. However, across the group we had a lot of experience of research and writing and some of us had encountered research on emotion before; that was enough to ensure that we were not likely to be 're-inventing the wheel' when we explored our own experiences in more depth. To put it another way, there was enough in our patterns of reflexive contextualisation and conceptualisation to suggest we had sufficient connections to the field to be able to intuit possibilities to add to it. That prior awareness may not be true for every group of collaborators or for every theme. For that reason, I would encourage less experienced researchers, or those encountering something that is truly beyond their frame of reference, to at least undertake some cursory engagement with literature early on. In doing so, the goal is to *touch on* the theme(s) of interest but not to dive too deep, since that could shut down the possibility of serendipitous interpretations emerging when engaging with the gathered empirical material.

6.3   IDENTIFICATION OF CONTEXTS

In relationally reflexive, collaborative autoethnography the first choice the group has to make is whether the study should look forward or backwards (or perhaps both) in order to locate suitable contexts. What I mean by that is to consider whether recollections or records of lived experience up to the commencement of the study are already rich enough to inform the work, or whether there is a need to gather material in the future with a clear focus in mind.

In our case, our motivation to progress the project on negative emotional experiences was heavily influenced by our past experiences. This led us to look back to the range of organisations and locations in which we had worked, over the length of our careers, to see if we could identify situations which 'spoke' in enough detail about the theme of interest. Of course, that was already likely to generate at least a partially positive response since we had identified the theme through shared conversation. However, there was always the possibility that our historical contexts did not have enough material, or that our memories (or personal journals) might have been unclear. In addition, a further reason for not focussing on past experience might have been that while it was rich in relevant and memorable material, we might feel it to be too personal or exposing to share. Overall, we concluded that our careers featured enough insights on negative emotional experiences that we were willing to share.

Being able to draw on past experiences had some benefits for reflexive practice. In particular, the benefit of using prior experience was the ability to 'go back to the site' as often as we wished and needed to, looking at the situation in memory again from the perspective of embodied and emotional reflexive practice, with the benefit of relational reflexivity to offer new views on how we recorded the details and constructed our stories. While we had fixed on this past orientation, it is interesting to note that as a group we came to construct our future-oriented practice differently (in similar situations to those researched), as the emerging insights from our study added to our scope of contextualisation and conceptualisation. This yields a second advantage of using prior personal experience in research in this way – it begins to support learning and adaptation during the process of working on the study, rather than depending on the finalisation of a formal contribution.

6.4   CHOICES ABOUT DATA COLLECTION

Our discussion about the contexts for our research had convinced us that our careers included incidents that could speak to our focus on negative emotional experiences. Engaging with autoethnographic/autobiographical experience in this way also gave us confidence that we would be able to describe our emotions authentically. However, this approach also has three potential problems, that we handled through working collaboratively.

The first potential problem is related to emotional and embodied reflexive practice. On the positive side (from a research perspective) we had no difficulty in identifying incidents for which we had strong memories of our emotional perceptions and even some recollections of interoception. Here is an example from the study, in which one of our authorial team describes his experience of struggling to handle conflict in a classroom:

> *It was getting ugly. At this point my throat was dry and I felt out on a limb. Not quite afraid, but completely uncertain and anxious about how to get the discussion back on track. I realised I had no idea, and just closed it down, asking (rather weakly) for students to reflect on these points privately, and offering to meet later in my office, with any students who wanted to follow these issues up. Everyone left, pretty much all were either upset or angry at that point.*

[The narrative continues after a meeting with two students, L and K, who were particularly upset]

> *I felt hollow and sick. Immediately after L and K had left, I called a trusted colleague, J, into my office. I wanted the support of a friend after an experience I had found tough – and to talk through the whole process while I was close to it, to understand how I could have handled it better and maybe intervened sooner or in*

different ways. I had a lot of questions buzzing in my head. J stepped into my office and I closed the door. I started to explain my experience, but I only got a few words out before I suddenly broke into ragged, sobbing tears, which surprised me – and shocked J. (Hibbert, Beech, Callagher & Siedlok, 2021, p. 16)

While the ability to easily recall such incidents was an upside, the downside – as the short excerpt above probably suggests – is that it could be painful to revisit these experiences and relive them. The primary emotional perceptions and interoceptive feelings are difficult in themselves; for example, the excerpt records experiences including a dry throat, feeling "hollow and sick", and unexpected sobbing. In addition, these feelings can also be accompanied by *secondary* emotions when relived and shared, such as a sense of shame or inadequacy in failing to manage the situation even if there is nothing that we could reasonably have done (Fein & Isaacson, 2009).

The focus of our research meant that we had to bring the primary perceptions and feelings into our reflexive practice, to become more aware of them and seek to explore them on another level. Staying with these primary perceptions was intrinsic to the study, but we had different levels of comfort in relation to the secondary perceptions and feelings. These may well have impacted on the kinds of experiences we shared (and would go on to publish). We did not delve into this tension and allowed, implicitly, each other to go no further than they felt comfortable.

The second potential problem is a rationally reflexive challenge. The experiences we shared were deeply contextualised into our self-understandings and expressed in conceptualisations that were also shaped by our life histories. On the one hand this is partly the point: it is the guarantee of the kind of authenticity that we were looking for in our accounts, so that we would be able to see ourselves honestly described in them. However, to accept (possibly) idiosyncratic authenticity is also to accept some limitations that come with that. One such limitation is that we were motivated to present ourselves in various ways that had some favourable aspect to them. The stories we selected as data all allowed us to present ourselves (at least at first) as heroes or victims, rather than villains or those with more complex or ambiguous roles in the stories.

Another limitation was in the nature of the stories, which were difficult to relate in summary form or to set boundaries around. For example, in the class conflict story mentioned earlier, the focal incident could in some ways be seen as the culmination of events taking place during a three-day intensive workshop or even a build-up of tensions across the whole year of a program. We found that presenting our incidents of negative emotional experiences left some of the contextualising action 'offstage', for both ourselves and readers. Careful summary scene-setting helped us to get around this problem, when we had explained our stories well enough that others in the group could 'get it' – at least well enough to enable conversation about it. This is a difficult balance, however, and later in the study it was tricky to find ways to present enough of our stories to engage readers and build on without amassing too much material than we could report in journal articles. The problem with this kind of poorly bounded material is that it does not always reduce to illustrative 'snippets' that are typical of studies that are more focussed from the start.

The third problem is a relationally reflexive challenge that connects with the need to help others to 'get it' when we are sharing our stories. It is concerned with how we select and present material that is likely to *resonate* with others, as well as being authentic. In some ways this is the relationally reflexive equivalent of saturation. The aim is *not* to have gathered data until new patterns or insights are tailing off, but to collate material until those who 'don't get it' become fewer and fewer. This required relational reflexive practice by including peer engagement beyond the team much earlier than would be likely in a conventional research study. We needed to pay attention to how the stories struck others when presented from our perspective (seeing how they were received), and how talking with others about their reception of our stories led to resolution around themes in ways that connected (or not) with our intentions. When we found that we were approaching a fusion of horizons in our understanding (Gadamer, 1998; Hibbert, Beech & Siedlok, 2017) we could have confidence that our material resonated with others. For our study on negative emotional experiences, we found that resonance was not difficult to establish.

Achieving resonance did not automatically mean that we had something interesting to say. It is quite possible to focus on general human experience without uncovering something new – and negative emotional experiences in themselves are pretty universal. So, there was a need to check for novelty too. As mentioned earlier, our research approach defers extensive engagement with literature, but it does not put it off forever. Relationally reflexive engagement with published scholarship had to follow, to explore how we received theoretical ideas as possible perspectives on our stories and how we resolved our ideas through conversation with the literature into a whole. The first stage of that process was to connect the broad theme more deeply to the literature and in doing so to ensure that there was scope for a contribution.

6.5 GROUNDING IN LITERATURE

Our connection with the literature in this case was already tacitly established, through earlier work involving most of the same group. In that earlier work it became evident that emotions had a role in explaining how we use reflexive practices in order to respond to a need to change (Hibbert, Callagher, Siedlok, Windahl & Kim, 2019). The emotions we focussed on in that study were positive rather than negative. However, the literature we engaged with in that earlier research also included some articles which touched on negative emotional contexts and circumstances in a very powerful way. In particular, Brown and de Graaf's (2013) work with terminal cancer patients showed how their research participants were able to make meaningful life plans through mobilising positive emotions, despite having to address overwhelmingly negative feelings first:

> *Managing future-time, through bracketing off bad-quality time and death, and/or living with more hopeful expectations, regularly involved tensions and paradoxes. Whether through enjoyment of the immediate short-term or the imagining of positive long-term outcomes, the looming presence of negative eventualities was seldom fully averted [...] Thus, managing futures through hope [...] inherently requires managing emotions – for oneself and for others [...]. Being careful with how one thinks, seeking to change how one feels, or expressing certain emotions and expectations of futures and not others, were each apparent within participants' accounts of their lived experiences.* (Brown & de Graaf, 2013, p. 557)

Being rationally reflexive after the fact, Brown and de Graaf's (2013) work was a strong influence on my own approach to negative emotions in the study that is the focus of this chapter. It was part of my contextualisation when reading new literature and also supported the motivation to engage with my own negative emotional experiences, which in turn was also part of the driving force for others in the project. Engagement with Brown and de Graaf's (2013) work in this way serves to illustrate a more relationally reflexive engagement with literature. Because of the resonance of the work (almost everyone knows someone affected by cancer: I lost my stepfather to the disease) we are more likely to receive the ideas offered and they are resolved on the common ground of experience. Thus, Brown and de Graaf were accorded 'trusted status' as academic partners in a literature-mediated conversation. I think this is true for any authors who create work that resonates with us, whether in academic writing or other genres.

Overall, there were a small number of resonant, pivotal studies that made a difference to the shape of the literature engagement, forming the anchor points to which the rest of the citations were tied. Such studies also used earlier literature in resonant ways which led us to follow up on those links. For example, Brown and de Graaf's (2013) study cited Hochschild (1979) on emotion work, which was particularly helpful. In addition, their treatment of negative emotions connected with the idea of *trauma* in another powerful work: Fein and Isaacson's (2009) study of how school principals had coped during and after mass shooting incidents in their schools. It is profoundly moving – if not shocking – to think that Fein and Isaacson were able to gather a *sample* of such individuals, but their account of the particular effects on the school principals is also powerful:

> *The emotion work of leaders in these school shooting sites was far different and exponentially more demanding than the emotion work of leadership in noncrisis times. In managing their emotions when facing loss and death while simultaneously trying to create a sense of safety and security for others, especially those closest to the epicenter of the crisis—paid high personal costs. The personal impact was profound. [...] Participants described how the stresses of post-shooting leadership sometimes contributed to divorce or strained family relationships. Many ruefully described how the needs of their families were often secondary to their commitment to professional duties. Although his wife had been diagnosed with cancer just days before the shooting, one participant, when asked to do so by the superintendent, agreed to serve as crisis team leader for the school district.* (Fein & Isaacson, 2009, pp. 1339–1340)

Similarly, reflecting on the long-term harm to school principals described by Fein and Isaacson (2009) led us to an engagement with Bessel van der Kolk's masterful book *The Body Keeps the Score* (2015) on post-traumatic stress disorder. All of these connections became important in contextualising and conceptualising our understanding of the struggle to contain emotions, which was a key theme in our study. Often these literature connections leaped over disciplinary boundaries. We took the perspective of Becker (1993, p. 220) on this point:

> *...qualitative and quantitative workers alike, have [...] just to get on with it, and take account of what must be taken account of to make sense of the world.*

In this way the core of our engagement with literature proceeded through 'conversational links' between sources either directly, or through the new conceptualisations that they offered for our ongoing work that suggested new lines of debate. In addition, I found it helpful to read widely on the themes that we had found in the stories of our experience, and I believe that we would not have come to the conclusions that we did if our habits had not included some *unfocussed* reading.

While the core of our approach to engaging with the literature was an open-ended conversation (or perhaps a curiosity-driven dialogue: see Hibbert, Siedlok & Beech, 2016) employing relational reflexive practice, it is important to acknowledge two caveats. First, the practice of resolution engages each literature source as a conversation partner; to do so honestly means engaging with insights that are challenging or discordant and not just those that are easy to connect to existing conversations, as exemplified earlier. This is not necessarily an easy task when reading, and even less easy when writing. For example, our study (Hibbert, Beech, Callagher & Siedlok, 2021) could probably have engaged with an alternative perspective on emotion regulation in some depth, but did not. Second, while following a conversational chain through and across the literature provided the most interesting ideas, we also 'fleshed out' our engagement with extant studies through a conventional sweep through recent literature in our focal area. This was necessary to make a connection to the likely outlets for publication and show that we had a line of entry to *their* conversations. However, while that literature sweep added some nuances here and there, it did not directly shape the most interesting insights from our work. I will return to that point later, after discussing our approach to analysis and theorisation in this study.

6.6   APPROACHES TO ANALYSIS AND GENERATING SHAREABLE INSIGHTS

Our approach to analysis was shaped around the principles I had developed with colleagues in a different and earlier collaborative project (see Hibbert, Sillince, Diefenbach & Cunliffe, 2014). That approach centres on relational reflexivity and while it uses different terms, the focus is on practices that resemble receiving and resolving. Table 6.1 provides an overview of the elements of the process, reframed to connect with the terms used in this book and to reflect the practicalities of the approach as it was adopted in the focal case discussed in this chapter.

Table 6.1   Relationally reflexive approach to analysis

Process element	Operationalisation in our study
1a. Developing plausible conceptualisations through Reception *(engaging otherness)*	Developing possibilities for our research focus and conceptual framework through exchanges between different team members.
1b. Developing shared conceptualisations through Resolution *(enacting connectedness)*	Allowing our individual contextualisations and conceptualisations to contribute to the refinement of a loose framework within shared horizons, leaving space for alternatives to surface in the processes of research.
2a. Developing theoretical possibilities through Reception *(engaging otherness)*	Listening to and reading personal accounts from others and interpreting them through our own practices of contextualisation and conceptualisation in order to explore possibilities connected to negative emotional experiences.

Process element	Operationalisation in our study
2b. Developing shared theoretical possibilities through Resolution *(enacting connectedness)*	Retaining data, interpretation and responses as separate yet linked aspects of our research conversation and withholding attempts to reduce these aspects to a consensus or 'superior' interpretive position in the first instance.
	A focus on developing resonance within the group.
3a. Refining and positioning theory through Reception *(engaging otherness)*	Dialogue on our contributions as both researchers and participants in our research, to flesh out plausible points of generative theoretical conversation within shared horizons.
	Later, reworking and re-writing ideas in response to conference feedback and friendly reviews that widened our horizons.
3b. Refining and positioning theory through Resolution *(enacting connectedness)*	Dialogue within the authorial team in collective meetings to 'join up' our theoretical conversation into an overall shared argument that was authentic for each of us.
	Discussion and dialogue with others beyond the group – through literature, in seminars, at conference settings and during review processes – in order to reshape our argument.
	A focus on developing resonance beyond the group.

I hope it will be a shock to no one that the elements laid out in Table 6.1 present an idealised version, with the actual picture being a little messier than that. For example, most of us will eventually encounter comments from reviewers that can push us much further back in the research process than we would expect (sometimes into re-analysis, or even additional data collection). In addition, there can be blurred boundaries between the elements shown in the table. Both of those possibilities were realised in relation to the focal study in this chapter. Nevertheless, the elements set out in the table do provide a useful way of organising and discussing our analytical and writing processes in the focal case.

As earlier parts of this chapter have suggested, to some extent the analysis began in parallel with the choice of research contexts and the kinds of material that we collated from our experience. We had already discussed and shared likely themes of interest at that point in order to know how to proceed, which set the initial conceptual framework for the research. However, this allowed some room for alternatives to emerge at any point. For example, early in our conversations we had focussed on leadership as a potential theme, but over time we shifted the focus to learning and then to self-reflexive learning in particular. Similarly, we had a general interest in negative emotions early in the study, before focussing in on negative experiences that were associated with emotion work (Hochschild, 1979).

Our openness to shifts of focus and direction came from working within a shared horizon, in which we understood each other well enough to go on with the study but did not seek agreement on every particular detail. To do this, we worked on shared notes and texts in a collaborative way, leaving comments and differences of opinion visible while we continued with our work. We developed alternative forms of diagrams to express our emerging theoretical ideas, and began to read more widely on emerging themes to enrich our conversations. Proceeding in this way during the early stage of the research (and into somewhat more formal analysis) required a certain generosity from those taking part. While there was a core of ideas that were resolved, many contributions remained in the background and could seem 'wasted'. This meant that there was a need for emotional reflexive practice, recognising that we might feel hurt when our ideas are not taken forward, and being alert to 'hot' motivations that might push us to seek to control the way the shared understanding is being shaped. The latter point was certainly true for me. For example, I think that the theme of leadership in the initial focus was strongly driven by my personal interest. I was working in a senior university management post at the time the study began and indirectly, I think, I wanted to understand and inform my practice in such roles, which can often include challenging emotional experiences of the kind that leaders are expected to contain (Dasborough, Ashkanasy, Tee & Tse, 2009; Lindebaum, 2017; Troth, Lawrence, Jordan & Ashkanasy, 2018).

Given our focus on negative emotional experiences that had 'stayed with us', it was inevitable that all of us had a significant personal interest in how our stories were handled. Thus, a need for further generosity and care was essential in the step that followed, which focussed on interpreting and questioning the stories that each of us had put forward. Trusting and caring relationships made it easier to receive interpretations that were at first difficult to handle, but nonetheless made sense when we explored them through our own contextualisation. For example, commenting on the classroom conflict story mentioned earlier in the chapter, one of my colleagues noted:

> *...the students' feelings of competition and anxiety [...] come from the structure of the intensive 3-day experience and the multiple tensions built in (no pre-work, client grading, random teams, last part of the MBA experience) ...* (Unpublished research note)

This triggered some key additional contextualisation for the author of the classroom conflict story, who mentioned in his response notes:

> *...in some ways the situation was primed for transgressive incidents. That ought to have been obvious to me, but I was too focussed on the traumatic imprint of the incident and not enough on the factors underlying it. This has helped me to think about how the nature of processes can lead to extreme 'emotional priming' and how approaches to leading through that can be developed. I have also been stimulated*

> *to learn from what was happening before emotions become obvious, and devote more time to managing the tone and 'temperature' of processes, and focusing less on outcomes.* (Unpublished research note)

The process of engaging with each other's stories in the study also helped the author of the story to recontextualise his own relational and emotional engagement:

> *...reading and thinking about others' stories (and reflections on their stories) [showed that what] we are ready to recognise in our emotions depends to some extent on how others are involved. That made my experience of speaking with J (in a 'relational place of safety' – so it's intuitively OK to cry) suddenly make much more sense.* (Unpublished research note)

Similar realisations could be cited from the accounts of the others involved in the study. In general, the initial themes that we used to develop our theoretical contribution came from key points of realisation that each of us had after hearing or seeing how others in the group interpreted our stories. We were able to receive their new perspectives, and resolve the different insights from ourselves and others into common themes. These themes supported a shared theoretical conversation that resonated for all of us.

Our theoretical conversation was enriched through presentation of early materials and more developed drafts at conferences, as well as continuing through the review process to publication. This is honestly how most qualitative research is developed, with some reshaping in response to commentary right through the process. Taking a relationally reflexive approach allowed us to be open about that. Engaging with anonymous reviewers was, however, a more delicate process. As is often the case, there were some helpful new perspectives but also some calls for layers and layers of precision around terms and interpretations that felt implausible for this kind of work. No one is ever going to be able to interpret autoethnographic material entirely for themselves and arrive at identical conclusions to the authors. That is why the study initially sought authenticity (so that the reader could believe that the stories come from life) and resonance (so that the conclusions reached would make sense in the reader's contextualisation of them) rather than direct generalisability. However, it was still possible to make a contribution to a wider theoretical conversation, through careful engagement with literature.

6.7   RECONNECTING TO LITERATURE AND READERS: WRITING INTO A CONVERSATION

There is a conventional boundary in most research approaches that separates analysis from writing, most particularly in relation to the discussion section of articles or similarly framed chapters in study-based monographs. However, things are somewhat different for a collaborative autoethnographic approach, centred on authenticity and resonance, that uses a relationally reflexive method. In such cases, the boundaries become blurred. Re-engagement with literature suggests new perspectives on the themes developed from the material, in some cases prompting a partial re-interpretation of the themes or suggesting a new way of making connections. A good example, mentioned earlier, is a shift in focus solely on negative emotions to consider how emotion work is involved in handling them.

Once the empirical material is re-interpreted, it can then suggest connections with other parts of the literature that may not have been as salient before, or alternatively lead to the elimination of literature that was previously important. A good example in the case of this study is the idea of transgression. In early drafts of our work, we considered that social settings and interactions that were transgressive (see Blackman, 2007) were important in stimulating or releasing negative emotions in our stories. Then, through iterative engagement with literature and empirical material, transgression dwindled in importance as ideas about trauma and the role of the relational context took its place in our argument. That is, however, a vastly oversimplified account of a messier process. Relational reflexive practices opened up new ideas for reception from across the literature, but since the literature was complex and rich with alternative and competing ideas, the resolution was often slow or provisional. The complexity of the iterative process also involved the different contextualisations and conceptualisations of the literature that the individual members of the group brought to the process, especially when we engaged with earlier studies that only one or some of the group were involved with. It was normal for us to engage in dialogue about how we understood particular aspects of the literature, on occasions disagreeing about possible interpretations, in order to resolve on a good-enough shared understanding to support a way forward.

We were also conscious, in our writing, to pay attention to cues about authenticity, plausibility and criticality that would at least help to shape and guide the readers' engagement with our work (Golden-Biddle & Locke, 1993, 1997). This included close attention to the 'shape' and style of articles in our target journal, including the balance of different sections and the ways in which claims of contribution were presented. Of course, this almost never works completely, as we would find out in the review process. But we had an insight into *why* it does not work from our own patterns of engagement. If a closely engaged group could still disagree (or have only provisional agreement) about how to express our connections with the literature, it would be almost certain that unfamiliar anonymous reviewers could find different perspectives too. I will pick that point up a little later, but for now I will mention that we sought to offset that disconnection from readers (with a view to connecting with practitioners as well as other academics) through presenting *ourselves* as well as our ideas through our choice of method:

> ...*the difference here is that we go beyond discussing our emerging theoretical ideas to discussing ourselves; that is, to allow practitioners to know something of who we are, why we think the way we do, and the influence of our peer community upon us. These are the questions implicit in every organisational research project (to greater or lesser degrees of focus on each aspect) and a true peer connection to the practitioners in our research context means that we need to allow them to 'research us' too. In this way the refined theory sits in an enriched understanding of context that is constituted by researchers and practitioners together...* (Hibbert, Sillince, Diefenbach & Cunliffe, 2014, p. 289)

If we had not been working in an autoethnographic mode as both researchers *and* practitioners and had instead conducted forward-looking research in new contexts, we would have sought to present ourselves *alongside* the work through workshops with practitioners in those settings, rather than seeking to do so solely through our writing. Either approach is somewhat exposing, and more than once I have experienced emotional perceptions about the exposure of personally troubling incidents (behind the most diaphanous veil of pseudonymisation) to the world at large. But this risky engagement is necessary in a process that recognises:

> ...*the constitutive role of conversations between researchers and the communities in which they participate. These conversations provide the basis for impact on overlapping domains of theory and practice [...and...] provide the means to extend beyond the obvious and immediate bounds of the research context.* (Hibbert, Sillince, Diefenbach & Cunliffe, 2014, p. 292)

Other than emotional perceptions associated with feelings of external exposure and vulnerability (Corlett, Mavin & Beech, 2019) and despite the explicitly emotional focus of our work, in comparison with the PhD research case study (Chapter 5), emotional reflexive practice was generally much less significant within the group during our re-engagement with literature and in our writing. This was probably because of our familiarity with each other, and the fact that while the study was important to us it was not a high-stakes landmark for any of our careers. It is also relevant to note the fact that we liked and respected (and still like and respect) each other. As my experience of some other collaborative engagements have suggested, where personality clashes or unbalanced relationships are involved, then emotional reflexive practice might be all too necessary. I am not going to cite examples at this point, both because the issues are not necessarily apparent in the published work and because there may have been flaws on both sides. In addition, while it is good to be cautious about new collaborative projects with unfamiliar partners, it is not necessary to agree with your collaborators on all points, since sometimes creative tensions can be productive.

6.8   RESPONDING TO CRITIQUE

The study in this case was unusual in including external critique *within* the scope of the methodology. As the opening story at the start of this chapter suggests, engaging with critique can be both helpful and frustrating at the same time. Nevertheless, it was expected that engaging with the comments of editors and reviewers, in the process of progressing the study towards publication in a journal, would lead to changes in how we moved from initial insights to fleshed-out theoretical contributions. That expectation was fulfilled and there were three important types of change that were stimulated. These pivotal changes can be thought of as relationally reflexive engagement with the reviewers, as we sought to receive their perspectives on our article and resolve differences with a new interpretation.

The first type of change was to how we defined key ideas within the theoretical background of our paper. On one level this is a familiar request for the clarification of terms, which can become tedious. One of the frustrations of academic writing is that everyday words can also be terms of art, which reviewers may ask you to clarify. We experienced some instances of that kind of frustration, where adding definitions would obstruct the flow of the paper and it was usually more helpful to delete terms or find alternatives. For example, at one point in a response letter to the journal editor and reviewers, we wrote:

> *We agreed with the need for more clarity in our use of terms. Accordingly, we have attended to this issue in three ways. First, we have carefully considered (following your advice and that of the other reviewer) whether all of the concepts that we used were really essential to our core argument, especially in the light of further re-analysis of our material. This led to the elimination of some terms [such as ...] and allowed us to focus more clearly on the remaining concepts.*

However, although it felt frustrating, this kind of 'pruning' was actually useful in making space for the key concepts that would be really helpful in establishing our contribution and opening up those ideas in more detail. In this case, those ideas were emotion work (rather than just emotions), self-reflexivity (rather than just reflexivity) and learning as a process of change that supports both authenticity and effectiveness. Because only a limited range of ideas can be received and resolved within a shared horizon of understanding involving three unknown strangers in a veiled, artificial and text-mediated conversation (that is, double-blind peer review), finding the necessary terms was important.

The second type of change related to how we presented our stories and used them to support our arguments. Writing and submitting qualitative work that relies on stories (even relatively short material of the kind that we used in our study) often leads to a challenge from reviewers, who wish to know more of the details of each narrative. This was the case in our study, accompanied by a request for a closer weaving of data and interpretation that "shows rather than tells". As is often the case, we found that combination of changes quite difficult to achieve within the length constraints of the journal. We took the decision to present one of our stories in much more detail than the others and organise the argument around that (*showing*), while reducing the other stories to summaries in a table that we would refer to for additional support or nuance (*telling*, but in a secondary and supporting way). Here is how we explained that change in our response letter to the editor and reviewers:

> *First, a simplified table (Table 2) in the methodology section provides an overview of all the stories, so that the reader is 'primed' to engage with all of the material that follows in the findings. Second, we have ordered the findings so that each section begins with Charlie's story, while allusions to the others follow later.*

Emotional perceptions are important when making the kind of change described above. This is because one of the group ("Charlie") was fore-grounded while the others were pushed into the background. This can trigger a mixture of emotions since it implies that one of the stories is richer or more persuasive than the others (leading to positive feelings for Charlie and negative feelings for the others) and it leaves one of the group more exposed (leading to negative feelings for Charlie and positive feelings for the others). This was not a difficult point for our group, but it might be troublesome in other cases, so it is worthwhile making space for emotional perceptions in the conversation when making these kinds of choices.

The final type of change concerned how we told the 'meta-story' of our research and articulated our contribution. It is difficult to present a linear narrative of an (often) iterative research process within the limits of a conventional academic paper. Over time, the review process tends to lead to a resolution that favours simplicity over precision. A good example relates to the location of the material supporting our first level of theoretical insights, which was a characterisation of four particular kinds of practice that were important in helping us to explain how learning from negative emotional experiences could become obstructed, and how those obstructions could be overcome. Originally, we had placed these descriptions in the findings which helped us to characterise them, but following reviewer input we placed initial definitions in the literature review section. Here is what we wrote about this change in our response to the editor and reviewers:

> *...we followed your suggestion that we should relocate the characterisation of the practices to the theory section of the paper. We originally felt – and still do – that the four practices were not all explicitly characterised in the extant literature while some implicitly were. Thus, the development of the characterisation is a part of our intellectual contribution. However, our stance on this was moderated by the fact that our reanalysis of the material suggested differences in the set, effectively eliminating and replacing one of them and adding nuance to (and renaming appropriately) others. While we felt that we would not have arrived at this revised set of characterisations without our engagement with empirical material, we also felt that the revised set could be more readily inferred from literature, with the benefit of hindsight.*

I have explained those changes as *types* rather than *steps*, to emphasise that they were not necessarily sequential. Indeed, one pivotal change in our paper came quite late in the process, in response to one reviewer's request for more clarification about what we meant by 'learning' in the context of our study. This request led me to re-articulate what I meant by the term, drawing on my own patterns of contextualisation and conceptualisation, in a way that the others in the group found helpful. Here is how we described this change in our response to the editor and reviewers:

> *We have enhanced the clarity of the paper in relation to learning, setting out a specific definition:*
> *...the learning that is enabled when emotion work is supported is concerned with developing an ability to act differently – to move on – and to 'be oneself' more authentically (Hay, 2014). This kind of learning is, therefore, a self-reflexive adaptation to our ways of being and doing. It changes our assumptions about, and engagement with, both our self and our world. (Hibbert, Callagher, Siedlok, Windahl & Kim, 2019)*

I mention my specific contribution to making this change as an example of how we were all engaged in rational reflexive practice in the midst of a wider relationally reflexive conversation. A relational approach does not generate ideas without specific contributions from the actual people involved in the relationships, whether present in person or being brought into the conversation through texts. However, the relational reflexive practices of reception and resolution provide a generous context for exploring, re-interpreting and selectively incorporating an individual's ideas in ways that make them useful for others.

6.9   OVERVIEW

As with the previous case study (Chapter 5), there are significant differences in the pattern of practices that played out in the study, as compared to the linear theoretical pattern set out in Chapter 4. The most significant difference is the divergent order of engagement with each of the elements of the research process, in an approach which differs even more than the doctoral example from most conventional qualitative studies. Added to this, there was less of a clear sequence of completion of each element. For example, some key definitions in the early part of our published study were some of the last parts of the writing to be settled.

The present case study also shares another characteristic with the doctoral case, in that the description of the application of reflexive practices is, albeit to a lesser degree, partly retrospective. That is because the characterisation of reflexive practices set out in this book was completed roughly in parallel with the study that the case focusses on. I could say, perhaps, that the two texts 'grew up together' – and I could not have written this book without working with my friends. Bearing in mind those caveats, the main structure of the research process and the incorporation of reflexive practices across this case study is summarised in Table 6.2.

Table 6.2   Patterns of reflexive practice in collaborative autoethnography

Element of the research process	Patterns of reflexive practice and opportunities for development
Characterisation, motivations and commitment	There was an initial *hot* motivation and deliberate, intensive engagement in relational reflexive practices in the context of trusting, friendly and non-instrumental exchanges, that became a *warm* motivation. The shape of the study was influenced by the additional insights received from each other and resolution through shared conversation. We felt that we had enough of a general view of the field to proceed with the study without bringing literature into the conversation at this stage.
Identification of contexts	We took the option to use a past-focussed approach, relying on the recall of emotional perceptions (and bodily interoception) through memory. This approach worked well since the explicit focus was on negative experiences that had 'stayed with us' and locating relevant situations in our past experience was not difficult.

Element of the research process	Patterns of reflexive practice and opportunities for development
Choices about data collection	Given the focus of the study, the ability to recall emotional and embodied reflexive practice were intrinsic to the identification of the (micro-) stories at the heart of the data. However, this also meant that we re-invoked the painful feelings within those situations. In addition, there were secondary emotional perceptions associated with self-exposure and rationally reflexive, critical challenges in relation to how we saw ourselves (favourably) within our own stories. Relationally reflexive challenges also arose, in the need for openness to widespread and varying patterns of reception and resolution, in order to ensure that our stories resonated with others in the ways that we hoped.
Grounding in literature	The rational reflexive practice of contextualisation made particular readings seem more relevant, when they connected with life experiences or our previous intellectual journeys. This supported a relational reflexive connection with the authors as 'trusted partners', from whom we were more likely to receive challenging ideas and with whom we were more ready to commit (indirectly) to resolution within a shared horizon. This also led us to follow their lead to other pivotal sources, through direct citations or bridging concepts. Overall, core literature was woven into a conversation that crossed disciplinary boundaries.
Approaches to analysis and generating shareable insights	The analytical approach was relationally reflexive (see Table 6.1 and Hibbert, Sillince, Diefenbach & Cunliffe, 2014). However, emotional reflexive practice was also important given the personal exposure in our stories and the significance of inclusion or exclusion that went along with this. A key question that arose was: how does it feel if a personal story of a troubling incident is seen as "supporting" or "secondary" rather than key material?
Reconnecting to literature and readers: writing into a conversation	Relational reflexive practice was expanded as the findings led to different readings becoming more or less salient. Some new sources were brought more closely into our conversation as trusted partners. Their connection to one individual's experience, through the work of contextualisation and conceptualisation, became apparent and led us to 'speak up for them' in the relational reception–resolution dialogue. We also sought to construct ourselves as likely (textual) conversation partners for readers through our authentic self-presentation.
Responding to critique	A process of relationally reflexive engagement with reviewers was afforded through the revision cycles of the publication process. The key challenge was to explore, establish and defend the limits of the shared horizon within which reception and resolution could be possible, when connecting with multiple anonymous readers through a distanced and obstructed communication channel. From time-to-time, this led to increased criticality through a formal requirement to 'open up' what was going on within our own rational reflexive practices of contextualisation (especially) and conceptualisation.

Wider relational dynamics were important in this case too, as in the earlier case (Chapter 5) but in two rather different ways. First, there is the issue of power relations. While there is always a power imbalance in favour of the decision makers at journals in comparison with the authors who submit their work, that does not mean the imbalance will have the same significance that it has for a PhD student completing their degree. Four established academic staff (some of us at the late career stage) had more freedom in relation to our publishing expectations and the case study project was, anyway, one of many for all of us. Our emotional investment in the project was more important than the symbolic achievement of where it was published, so had we not been successful we could have moved on to an alternative outlet (after dealing with the inevitable emotional perceptions, of course).

The more important influence of relational dynamics was tied up with the specific commitment to a relationally reflexive method. This enlarged our circle of relational reflexive practice to incorporate published authors as trusted partners, from whom we would actively receive ideas. At the same time, the method required us to seek to connect indirectly with peer critics, reviewers and editors as those who set the challenge for establishing the boundaries of the shared horizon of meaning, within which the resolution of all of our ideas into a coherent-enough whole might be possible. It is those two kinds of engagement that kept the whole of the process live, until the study was accepted for publication. While this model of research as conversation feels authentic and rewarding, it also has its frustrations and is not an easy option. Conversations are always imperfect even when direct, let alone through the indirect and somewhat formalised exchange of editors' and authors' letters. However, we were quite lucky in this particular case because the editor we worked with was sympathetic, engaged and thoughtful in his guidance.

In contrast, the *internal* conversation between mutually trusting authors in a group can function as a really effective environment for stimulating, noticing and recording reflexive practice. The traces in our interpretive comments on each other's stories, notes of meetings, photographs of exploratory concepts on whiteboards and marginal comments on draft papers all provided signals of this, which I could re-engage with when writing this chapter. To some extent this lessens the need (compared to the case with solitary PhD research) to keep a personal research diary. While keeping that kind of diary may still be useful (especially for personal learning), the group should provide a sup-portive and productively challenging context that supports recollection and evaluation of research experiences, as well as generating transitional material that records traces of those experiences. A powerful example of this is offered by Lehmann, Hansen and Hurme (2020, p. 832), in their study focussed on the terminal illness of Helena Hurme:

> *This process of collaborative reflexivity enabled a collaborative merging of existential meaning, acknowledging how sharing our stories with others, in the bonding vulnerability of our narratives, shapes the way we perceive life.*

To conclude this chapter, it is important to note one final similarity with the previous case (Chapter 5). That is, all of the types of reflexive practice were potentially active at any time during the study, but receiving less attention. The benefit of working in a collaborative group with a commitment to a reflexive approach is that collectively, there may be attention to different types of reflexive practice at the same time, or at least more opportunities for different perspectives and questions about what is going on.

Dialogue

1. This chapter has presented the case of a non-standard approach to research, but many of the issues and reflexive practice triggers will be common to other methods. What are the key differences and commonalities for you?
2. The research reported in this chapter involved a collaborative group in relatively secure positions; perhaps we could 'afford to be vulnerable'. How do we make safe space for others to be vulnerable in their reflexive practice?
3. It is probably apparent that the importance of working with friends has increased for me over time. I find trusting relationships important for relational reflexive practice. How does friendship figure in your research and reflexive practice?

7.   Conclusions and prospects

Looking back, many decades later, at my determination to be nothing like my father made me realise how central that had made him in my early life. Every sense of what was good and right was framed in relation to its distance from him; that was my main measure of how I should behave. This realisation made me grateful that I had also encountered many kind and interesting people over the years, friends and colleagues who had given me more positive impressions of ways to live. However, I think there are still things that I am working out, like a habit of observing and judging others, that come from those early years. I wonder if that also affects my approach to research...

7.1   THE CIRCLE OF REFLEXIVE PRACTICE

I wanted to return to the story offered at the start of the introduction in this final chapter, since it seems that looking back is a habit that often comes with reflexive practice. The more we develop in our life with others, the more insights we can retrieve and reconstruct from looking at our past. It is important not to be obsessed by that, but to see it as an expanding resource instead.

In this final chapter of the book, I am going to begin by briefly circling back to the contents of the preceding chapters in order to connect with the new insights that have developed from my own engagement in the writing process. Following the introduction, in the second chapter I began by undertaking a review of literature focussed on the concept of reflexivity itself and developing future-oriented and past-oriented characterisations. I then moved on from that conceptual discussion to consider how reflexivity is experienced and engaged with in practice, by considering embodied, emotional, rational and relational levels. My discussion of reflexive practice led to a consideration of how it is enacted in the context of research, after which two case studies explored some of my particular research experiences in which variations, opportunities and omissions were illustrated. One of the aims of presenting the material in that way has been to shift the focus from a clear theoretical debate to the more complex pictures of how we inhabit our research, both in the field and in the written outputs we use to record our projects. Overall, the arc of this book swings from theory to application, ending in cases which show that reflexive practice can involve making choices but is also, on some levels, inevitable.

In this final chapter, I build on the previous material in order to do three things. The first is to use the insights from the two case study chapters to 'talk back' to the earlier theoretical material, especially in relation to the initial treatment of reflexivity. I believe that there are some potential insights which can add to debates in this area and, furthermore, I hope that this offers a template for shaping your own ideas about reflexivity in response to experience. The second aim is to outline prospects for future research on reflexive practice, which (compared to the study of reflexivity itself) is a relatively under-developed theme in the literature. The final aim for this chapter is to dwell on the lived experience of reflexive practice in more detail. This final aim provides a very personal answer to the title of this book: it is my way of responding to the challenge of 'how to be a reflexive researcher'. I hope that my perspective on the challenge will feel authentic and resonate with you, even if your own response is different, so that we are within the same shared horizon of understanding.

7.2   LOOKING BACK AT THEORETICAL DEBATES

The overview of approaches to reflexivity in Chapter 2 included four main strands. First, self-reflexivity, the everyday processes of individual adaptation guided by our interpretation of experience (Archer, 2007; Hibbert, Beech & Siedlok, 2017). Second, critical reflexivity, which identifies the social constructions of tradition and ideology that shape our interpretations, to interrupt and challenge the norms we reproduce in this way (Aronowitz, Deener, Keene, Schnittker & Tach, 2015; Hibbert, Beech & Siedlok, 2017; Hibbert & Huxham, 2010, 2011). Third, relational reflexivity, which considers the interdependence of individuals, how our insights (may) influence others, and how they influence us (Hibbert, Sillince, Diefenbach & Cunliffe, 2014; Cutcher, Hardy, Riach & Thomas, 2020). Fourth, radical reflexivity, which builds on self- and critical reflexivity to deny robust foundational truths or easily generalisable insights about how we live in and interpret the world (Cunliffe, 2003). In addition, a counterapproach to radical reflexivity is offered by instrumental reflexivity, which uses the principles of critical reflexivity in a constrained and focussed approach, to remove less robust or persuasive insights about how we live in and interpret the world (Alvesson, Hardy & Harley, 2008; Weick, 1999).

A Different Integrative View

The approach to reflexivity and reflexive practice that I have elaborated in this book covers similar terrain to established approaches, in a different way. Self-reflexivity is given the primary position from which the other kinds of reflexivity are engaged. Looking *at the self* in relation to embodied and emotional experience is balanced with looking *from the self* through rational and relational engagement. It is in looking *from the self* that critical reflexivity is possible. This point of view does not, however, lead to a picture of the individual as a sovereign, rational and completely free agent. Instead, it overlaps with radical reflexivity through the ways in which rational reflexive practice acknowledges the limitations of contextualisation, that shape what is possible for us to describe in our conceptualisations, as well as expecting relational reflexive practice to disturb and expand our horizons of understanding. Only the *expectations* that flow from this approach have a substantial difference from radical reflexivity; rather than descending into a spiral of doubt (Cunliffe, 2003; Cutcher, Hardy, Riach & Thomas, 2020) we are expected to go on, aware of and living within our incompleteness and constraints. Even if we can never completely escape these limitations, we can seek to enlarge the boundaries. The perspective I have mapped out thus remains distinct from instrumental reflexivity (Weick, 1999) in its openness to engagement and influence from others, a continuing openness that expands our future ways of understanding rather than eliminating possibilities.

Another important difference of the approach I have set out is the focus on time; that is, the recognition that reflexivity can be either future-oriented or past-oriented. The future-oriented perspective follows, in the main, the work of Archer (e.g., 2007). This orientation of reflexivity always happens whether we wish it or not. It can be most obvious in embodied and emotional reflexive practice, since our bodily reactions and emotions often indicate an adaptive response to circumstances before we even recognise them. Think, for example, of the story of my flight home at the start of Chapter 3, or the reaction I experienced in relation to a particular research contact, as described in Chapter 5. Emotionally driven and embodied experiences run ahead of us sometimes. However, as the cases discussed in Chapters 5 and 6 suggest, rational and relational reflexive practice can also have a future-oriented role. That stance was intrinsic to the study at the heart of Chapter 6 (for the output from the study, see Hibbert, Beech, Callagher & Siedlok, 2021), which was focussed on learning from negative emotional experiences. The intent was to use rational and relational reflexive practice deliberately, to develop insights that would help us and others to avoid responding in the same way to similar challenging experiences in the future.

Despite the utility for future-oriented reflexive practice, Chapters 5 and 6 also clearly show the value of rational and relational reflexive practice for past-oriented purposes. Chapter 5 records instances of (and missed opportunities for) the full spectrum of reflexive practices – embodied, emotional, rational and relational – but it is at heart a rationally reflexive account of a particular research journey. I worked with documents and memory iteratively

to open up the contextualisation behind the interpretations that shaped my doctoral study, to consider how that informed particular conceptualisations and to
illuminate how those concepts, in turn, supported the development of outputs
from the research (for example, Hibbert & Huxham, 2010, 2011). In contrast,
the distinguishing factor about the engagement with the past described in
Chapter 6 (despite, again, the full range of reflexive practices being present)
was the reliance on relational reflexive practice. This supported an engagement
with the past in ways that provided the means for seeing it differently, through
interpretive work with others.

Researchers are often encouraged to 'build reflexivity in' to their practice
through formal techniques such as keeping a research diary day by day; that is
a sensible idea, especially if you are going to argue that you have eliminated
bias (as much as that is possible) through challenging your own position during
the execution of a study. However, my perspective, reached through writing
this book, is that we can also recover more than we expected through looking
back, especially if we work with others to look at our experiences in a new
light. The value of working with others cannot be overstated. In isolation,
our contextualisation will always be shaped by our individual formation and
will necessarily be partial, with some plausible interpretations being missed
as we go about our day-to-day research. For that reason, it is misleading to
assume that personal research records can help us to strip away distractions
from the truth of some matter. We cannot get back to something that was never
entirely there; it is interpretation all the way down (Gadamer, 1998; Hibbert,
Beech & Siedlok, 2017). However, relational reflexive practice opens up other
interpretations than those that might have been possible at the time, a process
which reveals new aspects of our stories that can help us to assemble meaning
in a different way.

Overall, then, I am arguing for an integrated perspective on reflexive practice in research that brings the different levels (embodied, emotional, rational
and relational) into a dynamic relationship that swings between the future and
the past, asking *what we should do next* in the moments and months of our
studies but also asking *how we came to make those choices*. Engaging with
reflexive practice in this way is more demanding than something like using
a particular intellectual tool, deploying an established methodology (although
I found having a framework for that helpful – see Hibbert, Sillince, Diefenbach
& Cunliffe, 2014), or committing to a recognised paradigm. I think that the
challenge goes beyond that and requires a commitment to what might be
described as a *scholarly way of life*.

Reflexive Practice as a Scholarly Way of Life

While frameworks help us and give some initial shape to our practices, in everyday research and life in general the boundaries are quickly blurred. As the case study examples in Chapters 5 and 6 have shown, while there are some reflexive practices we can expect to use in particular stages of our work, the need for others can emerge unexpectedly in particular circumstances. My contention at this point is that the more familiar we become with the idea of reflexive practice, the more an aware engagement with the full range of levels can become intrinsic to all of our activities. In the long run all of the practices – embodied, emotional, rational and relational – are 'on hand', but some are actively in use at a given time, while others are latent. Being aware of these patterns is not just about conducting studies, for those of us for whom research is a significant activity. It becomes intrinsic to a scholarly way of life, by which I mean an approach to understanding myself that recognises my essential incompleteness and partial perspective, a recognition that drives a commitment to learning and development. It is difficult to partition that approach into academic and everyday life; while I used to think that was a problem my view has changed (there: I demonstrated my commitment to reflexive practice!). In Table 7.1, I provide a simple summary of what everyday engagement with all of the reflexive practice levels looks like.

On the one hand it might seem odd to think about reflexive practice as you go about your daily life, attending to chores, enjoying your hobbies, and spending time with those you love. A scholarly perspective on this might seem cold and intrusive. It is certainly possible to misuse technical approaches to the detriment of the aspect of life we are seeking to enhance. For example, many people enjoy exercise, such as running, and attention to embodied reflexive practice through interoception is helpful to avoid injuries, notice how it makes you feel good – adding in emotional perceptions – and so on. But when the focus is shifted to rational reflexive practice, contextualising experience purely into medical perspectives with the aid of monitoring devices and deploying metric conceptualisations (how is my VO_2 max today? Oh no! It has dropped from 49 to 48!), it becomes both compelling and less joyful, directing us back into emotional perceptions but on an unhealthy trajectory.

On the other hand, there are some life affirming aspects to everyday reflexive practice. Think about what it means to accept that you will always be learning and changing (and that really is unavoidable, however hard you try), while at the same time recognising that no-one ever has a perfect perspective and/or can get everything right. It is quite liberating to realise that while your practices of contextualisation and conceptualisation have grown out of your formation in particular communities (Hibbert, Beech & Siedlok, 2017), you can still extend beyond these limits.

Table 7.1   *Everyday reflexive practice*

Reflexive practice	Focus of practice	
	Future orientation	**Past orientation**
Embodied, *Interoception*	Checking in with our bodies, especially at important decision points. Awareness of bodily signals and our adaptive responses in the moment, that affect what we might interpret on other levels.	Introspective thought about how bodily awareness/experiences impacted on past actions, noting whether the reaction was what we would choose or whether we would seek to act differently in similar situations.
Emotional, *Perception*	Awareness of emotions as signals of significant or critical events in the moment. Seeing these as an opportunity to note what is going on for later thought, or take immediate 'time out' to process, where possible.	Thinking, if it feels safe to do so, about experiences where emotions were significant and memorable but unexpected, with a view to exploring memory on other levels to work out what was going on.
Rational, *Apperception: Contextualisation/ Conceptualisation*	Awareness of the automatic link between contextualisation and conceptualisation: where interpretations will have a significant effect on our future, trying to slow this down in order to question our contextualisation.	Looking back at earlier interpretations, in the light of enriched possibilities for contextualisation made possible by subsequent learning, to generate alternative conceptualisations/ implications.
Relational, *Reception and Resolution*	Awareness of the possible insights that can be received from others as they arise. Seeking conversation when confronting ideas arise, to resolve meaning within a shared horizon of understanding.	Sharing challenging or confusing experiences with trusted friends or colleagues. Noticing what is received (by/from them) that is poorly understood and enlarging mutual learning through a process of conversation.

Think also about what a commitment to relational reflexive practice means to you in your most important, trusted relationships. It should lead to an appreciative disposition, recognising how much others have to offer us if we receive new ideas from their perspectives and resolve uncertainties to develop a shared horizon of understanding. In addition, because we are all in networks of relationships, those we trust are also changing and developing in the same way, in networks of other relationships. That means that what we can learn through friendships is never complete. That is an encouraging thought, but also underlines our responsibility to each other through doing our best to bring our reflexive, growing self to the relationship. We are all, always, responsible for ourselves and each other (Hibbert & Cunliffe, 2015).

Our responsibility for each other needs to be considered in relation to the risk, mentioned earlier, that reflexive practice might lead us into some unhelpful habits on a rational level. In addition, relational reflexive practice, built around trusting relationships, can cause concern when significant power inequalities are in play. That can lead to situations in which new ideas are received based on authority rather than accommodated through resolution in a horizon of shared understanding. We also need to recognise:

> ...*the ongoing challenge of remaining sharp in practice [...since...] it is not unlikely that we descend into our own particular complacent patterns and experienced habits.* (Winterburn, 2020, p. 232)

All of these kinds of risks point to a possible need for a different form of super-vision, in addition to the research supervision we may be familiar with from formal training and doctoral research. What is needed is akin to the clinical supervision provided to those in the caring professions (such as counselling, nursing, psychotherapy, and social work – see Henderson, Holloway & Millar, 2014) which focusses on *how* individuals are developing and growing in their practice, as well as helping them to work through incidents which have been troubling. This guidance might be provided through mentoring relationships, or by a mutually supportive group in an appropriate context (Parker, Racz & Palmer, 2020). For me, one of the positive outcomes *during* the study described in Chapter 6 was my realisation that the research group was provid-ing mutual mentoring, without that ever being stated or formalised. However, while the mentoring of *reflective* practitioners is well developed and has a rich literature, the mentoring of *reflexive* practitioners has not attracted the same level of attention. This presents an opportunity for further study, along with other emerging themes that also open up new questions.

7.3   LOOKING FORWARD TO NEW QUESTIONS

It is perhaps inevitable that any study of reflexive practice is likely to lead to new questions and opportunities for development. This is especially the case when new conceptual frameworks are assembled (Chapters 2 and 3) to develop a particular 'ideal type' approach to reflexive practice in research (Chapter 4), which is then used to review earlier research activities (Chapters 5 and 6) in order to see how the lived experience of research matches up. You may have formed your own opinion on the questions that have arisen from earlier chapters, but my personal take suggests two areas that present immediately interesting opportunities for further study. These opportunities relate to: the impact of personal health challenges on reflexive practice; and how reflexive practice is affected by institutional constraints and pressures. I discuss each of these in turn, below.

The Impact of Personal Health Challenges

If we are engaged in reflexive practice on every level, personal health challenges of a range of kinds may have an impact on us. For example, Frank and Solbraekke (2021) give a powerful and relationally reflexive account of the effects of their own and family members' experience of cancer, which affected them on bodily, emotional, rational and relational levels (and see also Lehmann, Hansen & Hurme, 2020). However, I am going to focus on mental health challenges, and in particular anxiety and depression. It has been established that there is a crisis of mental health in modern society (Ehrenberg, 2009). In addition, there is a particular problem in academia (Gorczynski, 2018), that has likely been exacerbated in recent times by experiences of the COVID-19 pandemic and its long-term effects on education and research (Greenberg & Hibbert, 2020). For those reasons, mental health issues deserve particular attention when thinking about researchers' reflexive practice. In addition to which, these are the kinds of health challenges with which I am most familiar and so I can connect with them most authentically. It is important to acknowledge that my experience will differ from others' and there are many mental health issues about which I have no personal insight, so the discussion on these points should be seen as tentative and is not a guide for practice. While there are arguments that reflexivity may support resilience (e.g., Winkler, 2014), if you have (or suspect you have) mental health issues and are not currently receiving professional support, I recommend that you seek such support before considering if and how any form of scholarly practice fits with your own approach to life.

A comparison of Chapters 5 and 6 quickly reveals that I felt a great deal more uncertainty and anxiety earlier in my career, during doctoral research, although there are other circumstances beyond the case studies where my anxiety was more acute and limiting. However, in relation to doctoral research, I imagine that anxiety on some level will be a common experience for many of us. I explained earlier that I related my particular anxiety at that time in part to a lack of experience (of both research and reflexive practice), as well as noting that I experienced it as a *symptom* of how I engaged in research rather than a *cause* of that pattern of engagement. But anxiety can also interrupt or have a more direct shaping effect on reflexive practice before engaging in research, especially if it is experienced to the level of an anxiety disorder. To illustrate the impact and possibilities that anxiety can bring, I am going to focus on a recent article which provides clear insider views on this experience and connects it directly with reflexive practice. Todd's (2020) autoethnographic article on researcher anxiety includes this quoted field note, which helps us to connect with his experience in a powerful way:

> *These were perhaps the hardest, most anxious days I've experienced before a set of research encounters. All sorts of scenarios ran through my mind – nobody would turn up, I would be so nervous, sweaty and out of breath that I would be unable to fulfil the sessions and would end up running out. Nobody would understand what I was trying to do, the logistics wouldn't work, I'd sleep in, I'd lose control of my muscle functions, my anxiety headache-migraines would deepen and set in for the whole weekend. I spent hours seeking re-assurance from family members and my partner. Anxiety seemed to cloud every thought and control every movement. Carrying this weary anxiety, I arrived at the tube station near to the workshop space. I felt as though I had been torched with an exhaustion so heavy that the work-shop looming ahead seemed like an impossibility, a distant goal I couldn't possibly reach ...* (Todd, 2020, p. 2)

Through the processes of his research, Todd (2020) came to the conclusion that his anxiety was a mediating factor in all of his interactions and that it had to be incorporated within his reflexive practice rather than screened out. As a means of presenting oneself authentically to others in the research context, this had some negative effects in terms of discordant moments but also positive effects in supporting trusting connections that were helpful for relational reflexive engagement. But his main point is to argue against the exclusion of anxiety from a reflexive account of experience. He argues that:

> *By describing anxiety as both a condition and an active agent which affects their bodies and bodily encounters across various spaces, places, and times, I further appeal to readers to push the boundaries of what is deemed acceptable to feel and embody in academia. Considering our own experiences of anxiousness (in relation to our selves, bodies, participants, the spaces of research, and the spaces and times of our everyday lives wherein anxiety is also felt), and folding these into our reflex-ive practices, writings and research outputs, I argue, is one means through which to achieve this repositioning of values.* (Todd, 2020, p. 17)

I very much agree with Todd (2020) about the need to enlarge what is consid-ered an acceptable range of feelings in academia (and touch on this in Hibbert, Beech, Callagher & Siedlok, 2021). However, there is also a need to consider how those feelings have certain effects, as well as what that means for our reflexive practice. For example, Khalsa and Feinstein (2019) explain that there may be harmful feedback effects on anxiety when interoception is inaccurate, which has the implication that embodied reflexive practice needs to be consid-ered carefully in such circumstances.

Depression will also have an impact on reflexive practice, and this may also have feedback effects on the emotional level. For example, recent research (Achterbergh, Pitman, Birken, Pearce, Sno & Johnson, 2020) has explained how an awareness of loneliness during depression can be associated with a vicious cycle of deepening depression, further isolation and increased loneliness. Is emotional reflexive practice unhelpful when that is the case? Physical issues, such as the effect of long-term, chronic conditions will also have an effect on depression (Wilson & Stock, 2019), which has implications for the impact of interoception and the practice of embodied reflexivity. Long-term chronic conditions experienced later in life may also have effects at other levels – rational and relational – since individuals may feel that these conditions impact on their sense of self. However, it is also possible that reflexive practice may have a role in helping us to adjust to such changes:

> ...*individuals with LTCs can experience a loss of their former self (if not diagnosed at birth/infancy) leading to the creation of a new identity with new restrictions which they then need to come to terms with [...] The importance of acceptance for improved mental health has been described. Across studies with individuals of varying ages, acceptance has been described as being at peace with the limitations and losses associated with the condition, acceptance of the condition as part of your identity, and being able to appreciate and recognise the life lessons learnt. Acceptance has been described as a gradual and difficult on-going process...*
> (Wilson & Stock, 2019, p. 1112)

While I see possibilities for reflexive practice in the context of mental health issues, I do so purely on the basis of the studies mentioned above, as well as having personal experience of anxiety and depression. As I emphasised earlier, my experience will be different from others' and should not be seen as a guide. For this reason, I think that there is a need for considerable further research on the relationships between reflexive practice and mental health issues. One possible focus could be on overlaps between reflexive practice and supportive therapies which work with and through awareness, such as mindfulness. Such studies could build on a limited amount of recent research, for example that focussed on the role of reflexivity and mindfulness in experiential and transformative learning (Tayar & Paisley, 2015; Vu & Burton, 2020). However, the breadth of reflexive practice, along with the continually developing literature on mental health, suggests that there could also be scope for a wide range of other studies adopting a variety of different perspectives.

The Effects of Institutional Constraints and Pressures

To some extent the situational pressures and institutional constraints that have an effect on the possibilities for reflexive practice have been discussed earlier, in three ways. First, critical reflexivity (Chapter 2) focusses on locating the social constructions of tradition and ideology that shape our interpretive practice, in order to challenge the unquestioned norms that we reproduce in this way (Aronowitz, Deener, Keene, Schnittker & Tach, 2015; Hibbert, Beech & Siedlok, 2017; Hibbert, Coupland & MacIntosh, 2010; Hibbert & Huxham, 2010, 2011). Second, this critical stance is reflected in the characterisation of rational reflexive practice and its movements of contextualisation and conceptualisation, especially the process of breaking the automatic link between those aspects of the practice. Third, the potential for relational reflexive practice to generate a new, shared horizon of understanding (see Chapter 3) can disrupt the previously unquestioned boundaries of our thinking.

The cases explored in Chapters 5 and 6 add to established debates by highlighting situations in which the ability to engage in reflexive practice to support a critical challenge, or at least the ability to report our experience authentically, is possible but constrained. The situations of doctoral research (as in Chapter 5) provide limited scope for forming really challenging opinions or taking radically different approaches. Even in later career stages, the obscured dialogue with reviewers in the processes of publication are weighted against authentic engagement. While there is always a power imbalance in favour of the decision makers at journals in comparison with the authors who submit their work, that does not mean the imbalance will have the same significance that it has for a PhD student completing their degree. Nevertheless, in both cases these constraints are structural and remain whether or not there is good will and a developmental, dialogic intent on both sides, which is often the case.

Other institutional constraints and pressures may be specific to particular research situations. Recent research includes some interesting studies in which specific situational characteristics affected reflexive practice, to the extent that the researchers have recognised and reported these effects. For example, Namatende-Sakwa (2018) worked on a study that focussed on homosexuality, in the wake of Uganda's anti-homosexuality bill. She explores the difficulties of being "…a Christian, heterosexual, mother, educator, undertaking a study on homosexuality, which is a thorny issue in Uganda" (Namatende-Sakwa, 2018, p. 328). She reports how she experienced her communities' challenges to her as a Christian and as a mother in undertaking the study, and the pressures which created a sense:

> …of failure, in my case, to live up to my family's expectations, and a sense of guilt that they will be associated with me – that my shame could have a ripple effect, shaming them too. I have thought of putting this research interest 'under wraps' – they needn't know about it, I have told myself – they might never find out. But again, supposing they do? It is this constant presence of fear as a feeling linked to the threat of rejection, admonishment, shame that creates a sense of anxiety which threatens to deter me from undertaking the study. (Namatende-Sakwa, 2018, pp. 336–337)

Understanding the pressures and constraints within a specific and distinctive situation, as Namatende-Sakwa (2018) did, can be difficult for outsiders. Thus, Anwar and Viqar (2017, p. 114) report on –

> *how the roles, reflexivity and positionality of our three Muslim female RAs [research assistants] adds depth to our understanding of fieldwork in a culturally and politically charged urban setting*

– in their field research in Pakistan. They explain how:

> *Kulsum's political savvy and common sense, Ainne and Sidra's sensitivity to the nuances of classed and gendered responses and reactions they both encountered and enacted in the field laid bare the political and social dynamics of the field for us in a way that we could not have experienced ourselves. [...] Our experiences have also revealed that the involvement of RAs occupying different social locations and attention to the interplay between their different subjectivities exposed biases and hitherto unknown aspects of knowledge production in the field.* (Anwar & Viqar, 2017, p. 120)

What is interesting too, is what Anwar and Viqar (2017) do *not* see, that they potentially could. For example, the RAs are not named in full (just first names), are not co-authors and do not feature in the acknowledgements list. In addition, the study reports – more or less – how the authors observed and corrected their RAs' biases and research practices. In addition, at one point the text suggests that one of the RAs was advised to demonstrate reciprocity to impoverished research contributors by offering to help female participants with domestic chores, rather than responding to requests for charity that the study authors considered undermined the ethical parameters of their research. I wonder what that says about the value of domestic work, as well as wondering how the RA felt about that. She certainly didn't accept the suggestion. These aspects of the study seem uncomfortable but let me emphasise that I am *not* judging the authors; I am simply reflecting that their text and their choices leave me with unresolved questions.

The two studies outlined above show how the particular situations in which we seek to conduct research (or go about our scholarly way of life) can impact on individuals on both sides of a power dynamic. Thinking about those studies and the cases reported in Chapters 5 and 6 suggests that those on the less empowered side might *struggle to say*, while those on the more empowered side might *struggle to see*. I have found myself on both sides of this divide. Further studies that focus on how we cross the divide, perhaps building on some of the ideas in my earlier work with colleagues (Hibbert, Sillince, Diefenbach & Cunliffe, 2014) seem to be called for, especially when considering our everyday scholarly life rather than how we address these challenges in specific studies.

7.4   HOW TO BE A REFLEXIVE RESEARCHER

Having staked my claim to an addition to theoretical debates and suggested some possible areas for new studies, I would like to conclude by responding to the title of this book with some practical conclusions about 'how to be a reflexive researcher'. There are four points that I would like to cover, in relation to: taking a theoretical position; becoming familiar with reflexive practices; developing honesty about our abilities and constraints; and being responsible.

Taking a Theoretical Position

As a reflexive researcher, you will be called to give an account of your theoretical position in your writing. I have provided an outline of the field, from my perspective, in Chapter 2, which I hope provides a useful way to engage with the possibilities. You could see the past-oriented and future-oriented perspective on reflexivity as one viewpoint and the different levels as another complementary viewpoint. However, you will find that other ways of categorising and integrating the field are available, and will doubtless continue to be developed – and your own integration will ultimately be the most useful to you.

The only counsel I would offer you is to avoid an overwhelming commitment to a particular paradigm. The philosophical paradigm purists have been having really detailed arguments for (literally) thousands of years and show no signs of coming to an agreement yet. In addition to which, if you sign up to a particular army in the paradigm wars, you are likely to miss a great deal of insightful work. For example, Cunliffe (2003, and later works) and Archer (2007) operate from completely different paradigms and some would find them to be incommensurable. Yet I have found both to be so formative and useful that I could not do without either. As I have mentioned earlier, I think that an interpretive research position can be seen as a 'universal receiver' – if you approach 'donor' insights interpretively, they can usually be incorporated in a variety of ways. My view on reflexive practice is also compatible with this stance: approach each review, article or monograph from a relationally reflexive perspective. Take from it what you are able to receive and resolve by crafting a shared horizon of understanding, write carefully about the kinds of claims you are developing from your mix of ideas and insights, and be attentive to the preferred rhetoric of your audience.

Becoming Familiar with Reflexive Practices

My core principle on how to be a reflexive researcher is that you achieve it by doing it. This is probably the one key point on which I differ from Ann Cunliffe, who tends to argue that you should work out who you want to be, and then decisions about what to do become obvious. To avoid one of those intractable paradigm arguments (see above) I will acknowledge that both approaches can go hand in hand. You can have an overall idea about who you want to be, but the things you do to become that person can play out in different ways and with different effects than you intended. This is inevitable since we are not fully able to control the situations of our practice, and those around us will interact with us in ways that are unpredictable. Above all, reflexive practice is about adapting in response to experience. How can that be possible if you have a fully fixed perspective on who you will be and allow that to shape a set of fixed responses, no matter what happens?

Familiarity with reflexive practices – paying attention to your embodiment, emotions, patterns of rational thought and relational insights – underpins an openness to change that accepts the inevitable incompleteness of our being and knowing. That openness sees the currently uninhabited spaces beyond our boundaries of knowing as room for growth, rather than a threatening void to be closed off with artificial certainties. Change will, at some point (if it is reflexive) involve a change in the practices that facilitated that pattern of growth. For that reason, even if it provides a useful starting point and you find it helpful for some time, I expect that in due course your growth will take you in a direction(s) that diverge from my framework of reflexive practices. Perhaps you will develop a more holistic perspective, integrate from a different starting point, or focus on the blurred boundaries and overlaps rather than discrete levels. Or, perhaps, you have already developed your own pattern of practice, that I will discover in my future reading. In any case, expect change: practice always ends up running ahead of theory.

Developing Honesty about Abilities and Constraints

Accepting our incompleteness and the mutability of our practices over time helps us to be honest about the limits of our abilities and reflect on the constraints within which we can grow and change. One of the major philosophers and scholars of hermeneutics of the last hundred years, Hans Georg Gadamer, is reported as remarking that it is the soul of hermeneutics that the other person may be right (Grondin, 2011, alludes to this in general terms). Similarly, reflexive researchers living a scholarly way of life expect to encounter others who have more fitting insights for the situations we encounter than those we bring ourselves. Our individual formational trajectories can close off lines of sight as well as opening up new vistas, which is why working with others on shared horizons of understanding is so helpful in maintaining and building a breadth of understanding.

Going beyond a broad-brush perspective on our limited perspectives, we may also have different capacities and abilities in relation to some levels of reflexive practice. Some are more or less accurate in their interoceptive abilities. Emotional awareness – in relation to oneself and others – comes easily to some and not to others. Differences in our formational journeys may provide some with more scope for contextualisation of experience than others, in addition to which we may be more or less fluent in relational engagement with others who are quite different from ourselves. It is likely that few of us will find reflexive practice easy on all levels, so it is good to be aware of where our limitations lie. Once again, working with others is likely to help, both in terms of developing an awareness of our limitations and in working, collectively, to offset them.

Acknowledgement of situational constraints is also helpful. Earlier in this chapter I mentioned some studies, from Anwar and Viqar (2017) and Namatende-Sakwa (2018) that help to show how our different situations can impact on what we can see or say. In addition to such long-term situational constraints in research, there are also the constraints on everyday practice from our relentlessly busy and fractured lives. If attention to reflexive practice (especially commitment to the use of writing methods to capture it) just adds to your agenda when you are already exhausted: give yourself a break. All of us in academic careers are notorious for over-commitment and we need to be careful about that. Instead, a scholarly way of life has to be approached like an athletic career. What I mean by that is if your practice hurts: stop, rest and re-evaluate.

Being Responsible

My final thought on 'how to be a reflexive researcher' is a brief one. I have emphasised multiple times throughout this chapter, and the book as a whole, the value of working with others. As we engage with others we are entering into their situations and their reflexive practice too; indeed, this is a normal and inescapable aspect of everyday living and is not just a characteristic of a scholarly way of life. What we do and say and how we act can have an impact on others, in ways that we cannot know in advance, and that is also true for the impact of others on us. It is therefore imperative that we remember to care for and about ourselves and others, in our pursuit of reflexive practice.

Dialogue

1. This chapter includes a summary of how the four levels of reflexive practice may look in everyday life as well as research, but I have not focussed on when and how the insights from them could be captured. How would you go about that?
2. I have suggested two possible areas for additional detailed research on reflexivity and reflexive practice, but there will undoubtedly be others. What themes for research would you add to the mix?
3. I emphasise the need for responsibility and care – for ourselves and others – that flows from understanding and committing to reflexive practice. How does that play out in your research situations and everyday life?

References

Abell, P. 2004. Narrative explanation: An alternative to variable-centred explanation? *Annual Review of Sociology*, 30: 287–310.

Achterbergh, L., Pitman, A., Birken, M., Pearce, E., Sno, H. & Johnson, S. 2020. The experience of loneliness among young people with depression: A qualitative meta-synthesis of the literature. *BMC Psychiatry*, 20: Article 415.

Adjepong, A. 2019. Invading ethnography: A queer of color reflexive practice. *Ethnography*, 20: 27–46.

Ajjawi, R., Hilder, J., Noble, C., Teodorczuk, A. & Billett, S. 2020. Using video-reflexive ethnography to understand complexity and change practice. *Medical Education*, online, doi: 10.1111/medu.14156.

Allen, M. & Tsakiris, M. 2019. The body as first prior: Interoceptive predictive processing and the primacy of self-models. In: Tsakiris, M. & De Preester, H. (eds.), *The Interoceptive Mind*, pp. 27–45. Oxford: Oxford University Press.

Allen, S. 2017. Learning from friends: Developing appreciations for unknowing in reflexive practice. *Management Learning*, 48: 125–139.

Allen, S., Cunliffe, A.L. & Easterby-Smith, M. 2019. Understanding sustainability through the lens of ecocentric radical-reflexivity: Implications for management education. *Journal of Business Ethics*, 154: 781–795.

Alvesson, M. 2003. Beyond neopositivists, romantics and localists: A reflexive approach to interviews in organizational research. *Academy of Management Review*, 28: 13–33.

Alvesson, M., Hardy, C. & Harley, B. 2008. Reflecting on reflexivity: Reflexive textual practices in organization and management theory. *Journal of Management Studies*, 45: 480–501.

Alvesson, M. & Skoldberg, K. 2000. *Reflexive Methodology: New Vistas for Qualitative Research*. London: Sage.

Anwar, N. & Viqar, S. 2017. Research assistants, reflexivity and the politics of fieldwork in urban Pakistan. *Area*, 49: 114–121.

Archer, M. 2007. *Making Our Way Through the World*. Cambridge: Cambridge University Press.

Aronowitz, R., Deener, A., Keene, D., Schnittker, J. & Tach, L. 2015. Cultural reflexivity in health research and practice. *American Journal of Public Health*, 105(S3): S403–S408.

Ashkanasy, N. 2003. Emotions in organizations: A multilevel perspective. In: Dansereau, F. & Yammarino, F. (eds.), *Research in Multi-Level Issues: Multi-Level Issues in Organizational Behavior and Strategy*, Vol. 2, pp. 9–54. Bingley: Emerald.

Ayas, K. 2003. Managing action and research for rigor and relevance: The case of Fokker Aircraft. *Human Resource Planning*, 26(2): 19–29.

Babo-Rebelo, M. & Tallon-Baudry, C. 2019. Interoceptive signals, brain dynamics and subjectivity. In: Tsakiris, M. & De Preester, H. (eds.), *The Interoceptive Mind*, pp. 46–62. Oxford: Oxford University Press.

Becker, H. 1993. Theory: The necessary evil. In: Flinders, D. & Mills, G. (eds.), *Theory and Concepts in Qualitative Research: Perspectives from the Field*, pp. 218–229. New York: Teachers College Press.

Beech, N., Gilmore, C., Hibbert, P. & Ybema, S. 2016. Identity-in-the-work and musicians' struggles: The production of self-questioning identity work. *Work, Employment and Society*, 30: 506–522.

Beech, N., Hibbert, P., McInnes, P. & MacIntosh, R. 2009. 'But I thought we were friends?' Life cycles and research relationships. In: Ybema, S., Yanow, D., Wels, H. & Kamsteeg, F. (eds.), *Organizational Ethnography*, pp. 196–214. London: Sage.

Beech, N., Linstead, A. & Sims, D. (eds.) 2007. *Researching Identity: Concepts and Methods*. London: Routledge.

Bell, E. 2010. The elephant in the room: Critical management studies as a site of body pedagogics. *Management Learning*, 41: 429–442.

Berntson, G., Gianaros, P. & Tsakiris, M. 2019. Interoception and the autonomic nervous system: Bottom-up meets top-down. In: Tsakiris, M. & De Preester, H. (eds.), *The Interoceptive Mind*, pp. 3–23. Oxford: Oxford University Press.

Bissett, N. & Saunders, S. 2015. Criticality and collegiality: A method for humanizing everyday practice? *Journal of Management Education*, 39: 597–625.

Blackman, S.J. 2007. 'Hidden ethnography': Crossing emotional borders in qualitative accounts of young people's lives. *Sociology*, 41: 699–716.

Boje, D.M., Luhman, J.T. & Baack, D.E. 1999. Hegemonic stories and encounters between storytelling organisations. *Journal of Management Inquiry*, 8: 340–360.

Boncori, I. & Smith, C. 2019. I lost my baby today: Embodied writing and learning in organizations. *Management Learning*, 50: 74–86.

Bourdieu, P. 2004. *Science of Science and Reflexivity*. Cambridge: Polity.

Brown, D. 2004. *Tradition and Imagination*. Oxford: Oxford University Press.

Brown, P. & de Graaf, S. 2013. Considering a future which may not exist: The construction of time and expectations amidst advanced-stage cancer. *Health, Risk & Society*, 15: 543–560.

Burkitt, I. 2012. Emotional reflexivity: Feeling, emotion and imagination in reflexive dialogues. *Sociology*, 46: 458–472.

Caetano, A. 2017. Coping with life: A typology of personal reflexivity. *The Sociological Quarterly*, 58: 32–50.

Caffrey, L., Ferlie, E. & McKevitt, C. 2019. The strange resilience of new public management: The case of medical research in the UK's national health service. *Public Management Review*, 21: 537–558.

Callagher, L., El Sahn, Z., Hibbert, P., Korber, S. & Siedlok, F. 2021. Early career researchers' identity threats in the field: The shelter and shadow of collective support. *Management Learning*, online, doi: 10.1177/1350507621997738.

Cassell, C., Radcliffe, L. & Malik, F. 2020. Participant reflexivity in organizational research design. *Organizational Research Methods*, 23: 750–773.

Chilvers, J. & Kearnes, M. 2020. Remaking participation in science and democracy. *Science, Technology, & Human Values*, 45: 347–380.

Clarke, D.W. 2017. Fighting against forgetting: Remembering the places where my relationship with my father came into being. *Qualitative Inquiry*, 23: 473–477.

Collien, I. 2018. Critical–reflexive–political: Dismantling the reproduction of dominance in organisational learning processes. *Management Learning*, 49: 131–149.

Corlett, S. 2013. Participant learning in and through research as reflexive dialogue: Being 'struck' and the effects of recall. *Management Learning*, 44: 453–469.

Corlett, S., Mavin, S. & Beech, N. 2019. Reconceptualizing vulnerability and its value for managerial identity and learning. *Management Learning*, 50: 556–575.

Critchley, H. & Harrison, N. 2013. Visceral influences on brain and behavior. *Neuron*, 77: 624–638.

Cropper, S., Ebers, M., Huxham, C. & Ring, P. (eds.) 2008. *Handbook of Interorganizational Relations*. Oxford: Oxford University Press.

Cunliffe, A.L. 2002. Reflexive dialogical practice in management learning. *Management Learning*, 33: 35–61.

Cunliffe, A.L. 2003. Reflexive inquiry in organizational research: Questions and possibilities. *Human Relations*, 56: 983–1003.

Cunliffe, A.L. 2004. On becoming a critically reflexive practitioner. *Journal of Management Education*, 28: 407–426.

Cunliffe, A.L. 2011. Crafting qualitative research: Morgan and Smircich 30 years on. *Organizational Research Methods*, 14: 647–673.

Cunliffe, A.L. & Jun, J.S. 2005. The need for reflexivity in public administration. *Administration and Society*, 37: 225–242.

Cunliffe, A.L. & Karunanayake, G. 2013. Working within hyphen-spaces in ethnographic research: Implications for research identities and practice. *Organizational Research Methods*, 16: 364–392.

Cutcher, L., Hardy, C., Riach, K. & Thomas, R. 2020. Reflections on reflexive theorizing: The need for a little more conversation. *Organization Theory*, 1: 1–28.

Danchev, A. 2011. *On Art and War and Terror*. Edinburgh: Edinburgh University Press.

Dasborough, M., Ashkanasy, N., Tee, E. & Tse, H. 2009. What goes around comes around: How meso-level negative emotional contagion can ultimately determine organizational attitudes toward leaders. *Leadership Quarterly*, 20: 571–585.

Davey, N. 2006. *Unquiet Understanding*. Albany: State University of New York Press.

Davey, N. 2011. Philosophical hermeneutics: An education for all seasons? In: Fairfield, P. (ed.), *Education, Dialogue and Hermeneutics*, pp. 39–60. London: Continuum.

Davey, N. 2013. *Unfinished Worlds: Hermeneutics, Aesthetics and Gadamer*. Edinburgh: Edinburgh University Press.

Davies, J., McGregor, F. & Horan, M. 2019. Autoethnography and the doctorate in business administration: Personal, practical and scholarly impacts. *International Journal of Management Education*, 17: 201–213.

Deetz, S.A. 1996. Describing differences in approaches to organization science: Rethinking Burrell and Morgan and their legacy. *Organization Science*, 7: 191–207.

Derrida, J. 1976. *Of Grammatology* (G.C. Spivak, Trans.). Baltimore, MD: Johns Hopkins University Press.

Derrida, J. 1978. *Writing and Difference*. Chicago: University of Chicago Press.

Driver, M. 2015. How trust functions in the context of identity work. *Human Relations*, 68: 899–923.

Dutton, D.G. & Aron, A.P. 1974. Some evidence for heightened sexual attraction under conditions of high anxiety. *Journal of Personality and Social Psychology*, 30: 510–517.

Eden, C. & Huxham, C. 1996. Action research for management research. *British Journal of Management*, 7: 75–86.

Edmondson, A.C. & McManus, S.E. 2007. Methodological fit in management field research. *Academy of Management Review*, 32: 1155–1179.

Ehrenberg, A. 2009. *Weariness of the Self: Diagnosing the History of Depression in the Contemporary Age*. Montreal: McGill-Queen's Press.

Epstein, R.A. 2016. Linguistic relativism and the decline of the rule of law. *Harvard Journal of Law & Public Policy*, 39: 583–630.

Eriksen, M., Van Echo, K., Harmel, A., Kane, J., Curran, K., Gustafson, G. & Shults, R. 2005. Conceptualizing and engaging in organizational change as an embodied experience within a practical reflexivity community of practice: Gender performance at the U.S. Coast Guard Academy. *Tamara*, 4: 75–80.

Evans, R., Ribbens McCarthy, J., Bowlby, S., Wouangoa, J. & Kébé, F. 2017. Producing emotionally sensed knowledge? Reflexivity and emotions in researching responses to death. *International Journal of Social Research Methodology*, 20: 585–598.

Fairfield, P. 2011. Dialogue in the classroom. In: Fairfield, P. (ed.), *Education, Dialogue and Hermeneutics*, pp. 77–90. London: Continuum.

Fein, A. & Isaacson, N. 2009. Echoes of Columbine: The emotion work of leaders in school shooting sites. *American Behavioral Scientist*, 52: 1327–1346.

Ferlie, E., Fitzgerald, L., Wood, M. & Hawkins, C. 2005. The nonspread of innovations: The mediating role of professionals. *Academy of Management Journal*, 48: 117–134.

Fernando, M., Reveley, J. & Learmonth, M. 2020. Identity work by a non-white immigrant business scholar: Autoethnographic vignettes of covering and accenting. *Human Relations*, 73: 765–788.

Fotopolou, A. & Tsakiris, M. 2017. Mentalizing homeostasis: The social origins of interoceptive inference. *Neuropsychoanalysis*, 19: 3–28.

Frank, A.W. & Solbraekke, K.N. 2021. Becoming a cancer survivor: An experiment in dialogical health research. *Health*, online, doi: 10.1177/13634593211005178.

Gadamer, H-G. 1998. *Truth and Method*, revised 2nd edition. New York: Continuum.

Galibert, C. 2004. Some preliminary notes on actor–observer anthropology. *International Social Science Journal*, 56: 455–466.

Gallagher, S. 2000. Philosophical conceptions of the self: Implications for cognitive science. *Trends in Cognitive Science*, 4: 14–21.

Garrety, K., Badham, R., Morrigan, V., Rifkin, W. & Zanko, M. 2003. The use of personality typing in organizational change: Discourse, emotions and the reflexive subject. *Human Relations*, 56: 211–235.

Gill, M. 2014. The possibilities of phenomenology for organizational research. *Organizational Research Methods*, 17: 118–137.

Gille, Z. & Riain, S. 2002. Global ethnography. *Annual Review of Sociology*, 28: 271–295.

Gilmore, S. & Kenny, K. 2015. Work-worlds colliding: Self-reflexivity, power and emotion in organizational ethnography. *Human Relations*, 68: 55–78.

Gioia, D.A., Corley, K.G. & Hamilton, A.L. 2012. Seeking qualitative rigor in inductive research: Notes on the Gioia methodology. *Organizational Research Methods*, 16: 15–31.

Golden-Biddle, K. & Locke, K. 1993. Appealing work: An investigation of how ethnographic texts convince. *Organization Science*, 4: 595–616.

Golden-Biddle, K. & Locke, K. 1997. *Composing Qualitative Research*. Thousand Oaks, CA: Sage.

Gorczynski, P. 2018. More academics and students have mental health problems than ever before. *The Conversation*, 22 February, online, https:// theconversation.com/more-academics-and-students-have-mental-health-problems-than- ever-before-90339.

Grahle, C. & Hibbert, P. 2020. Ethnography of creativity: Looking through a practice lens. In: Dörfler, V. & Stierand, M. (eds.), *Handbook of Research Methods on*

Creativity, pp. 184–193. Cheltenham, UK and Northampton, MA, USA: Edward Elgar Publishing.

Gray, B. 2008. Putting emotion and reflexivity to work in researching migration. *Sociology*, 42: 935–952.

Greenberg, D. & Hibbert, P. 2020. Learning to hope and hoping to learn. *Academy of Management Learning & Education*, 19: 123–130.

Grondin, J. 2011. Gadamer's experience and theory of education: Learning that the other may be right. In: Fairfield, P. (ed.), *Education, Dialogue and Hermeneutics*, pp. 5–20. London: Continuum.

Habermas, J. 1987a. *The Theory of Communicative Action Vol I: Reason and the Rationalization of Society*. Cambridge: Polity.

Habermas, J. 1987b. *The Theory of Communicative Action Vol II: The Critique of Functionalist Reason*. Cambridge: Polity.

Hardy, B. & Hibbert, P. 2012. Interaction, introspection and interoception: Listening to the body's voice in reflexive incidents. Presented to the Academy of Management Conference, Boston, USA.

Hay, A. 2014. 'I don't know what I am doing!': Surfacing struggles of managerial identity work. *Management Learning*, 45: 509–524.

Henderson, P., Holloway, J. & Millar, A. 2014. *Practical Supervision*. London: Jessica Kingsley.

Heracleous, C. 2001. An ethnographic study of culture in the context of organizational change. *Journal of Applied Behavioural Science*, 37: 426–446.

Hibbert, P. 2013. Approaching reflexivity through critical reflection: Issues for critical management education. *Journal of Management Education*, 37: 803–827.

Hibbert, P., Beech, N., Callagher, L. & Siedlok, F. 2021. After the pain: Reflexive practice, emotion work and learning. *Organization Studies*, online, doi: 10.1177/01708406211011014.

Hibbert, P., Beech, N. & Siedlok, F. 2017. Leadership formation: Interpreting experience. *Academy of Management Learning & Education*, 16: 603–622.

Hibbert, P., Callagher, L., Siedlok, F., Windahl, C. & Kim, H-S. 2019. (Engaging or avoiding) responsibility through reflexive practices. *Journal of Management Inquiry*, 28: 187–203.

Hibbert, P., Coupland, C. & MacIntosh, R. 2010. Reflexivity: Recursion and relationality in organizational research processes. *Qualitative Research in Organizations and Management*, 5: 47–62.

Hibbert, P. & Cunliffe, A. 2015. Responsible management: Engaging moral reflexive practice through threshold concepts. *Journal of Business Ethics*, 127: 177–188.

Hibbert, P. & Huxham, C. 2010. The past in play: Tradition in the structures of collaboration. *Organization Studies*, 31: 525–554.

Hibbert, P. & Huxham, C. 2011. The carriage of tradition: Knowledge and its past in network contexts. *Management Learning*, 42: 7–24.

Hibbert, P., Huxham, C. & Ring, P. 2008. Managing collaborations. In: Cropper, S., Ebers, M., Huxham, C. & Ring, P. (eds.), *Handbook of Interorganizational Relations*, pp. 390–416. Oxford: Oxford University Press.

Hibbert, P., MacIntosh, R. & McInnes, P. 2007. Identity trajectories in participative organizational research. In: Beech, N., Linstead, A. & Sims, D. (eds.), *Researching Identity: Concepts and Methods*, pp. 237–250. London: Routledge.

Hibbert, P., Siedlok, F. & Beech, N. 2016. The role of interpretation in learning practices, in the context of collaboration. *Academy of Management Learning & Education*, 15: 26–44.

Hibbert, P., Sillince, J., Diefenbach, T. & Cunliffe, A. 2014. Relationally reflexive practice: A generative approach to theory development in qualitative research. *Organizational Research Methods*, 17: 278–298.

Hochschild, A. 1979. Emotion work, feeling rules, and social structure. *American Journal of Sociology*, 85: 551–575.

Holland, R. 1999. Reflexivity. *Human Relations*, 52: 463–484.

Holmes, M. 2010. The emotionalization of reflexivity. *Sociology*, 44: 139–154.

Humphreys, M., Brown, A. & Hatch, M. 2003. Is ethnography jazz? *Organization*, 10: 5–31.

Huxham, C. & Hibbert, P. 2011. Use matters ... and matters of use: Building theory for reflective practice. *Public Management Review*, 13: 273–291.

Huxham, C. & Vangen, S. 2005. *Managing to Collaborate*. London: Routledge.

Immordino-Yang, M. 2016. *Emotions, Learning and the Brain*. New York: W.W. Norton & Company.

Irving, G. Wright, A. & Hibbert, P. 2019. Threshold concept learning: Emotions and liminal space transitions. *Management Learning*, 50: 355–373.

Iszatt-White, M., Kempster, S. & Carroll, B. 2017. An educator's perspective on reflexive pedagogy: Identity undoing and issues of power. *Management Learning*, 48: 582–596.

Jost, J. & Hunyady, O. 2005. Antecedents and consequences of system-justifying ideologies. *Current Directions in Psychological Science*, 14: 260–265.

Kearney, R. 2002. *On Stories*. London: Routledge.

Keevers, L. & Treleaven, L. 2011. Organizing practices of reflection: A practice-based study. *Management Learning*, 42: 505–520.

Khalsa, S. & Feinstein, J. 2019. The somatic error hypothesis of anxiety. In: Tsakiris, M. & De Preester, H. (eds.), *The Interoceptive Mind*, pp. 144–164. Oxford: Oxford University Press.

Kilduff, M. & Mehra, A. 1997. Postmodernism and organizational research. *Academy of Management Review*, 22: 453–481.

Kock, N. 2004: The three threats of action research: A discussion of methodological antidotes in the context of an information systems study. *Decision Support Systems*, 37: 265–286.

Kogler, H. 1999. *The Power of Dialogue; Critical Hermeneutics After Gadamer and Foucault*. Cambridge, MA: MIT Press.

Laing, C. & Moules, N. 2014. Stories from cancer camp: Tales of glitter and gratitude. *Journal of Applied Hermeneutics*, 31 January 2014: Article 3.

Laing, C., Moules, N., Sinclair, S. & Estefan, A. 2020. Understanding the impact on healthcare professionals of viewing digital stories of adults with cancer: A hermeneutic study. *Journal of Applied Hermeneutics*, 2020: Article 1.

Lambrechts, F., Grieten, S., Bouwen, R. & Corthouts, F. 2009. Process consultation revisited: Taking a relational practice perspective. *The Journal of Applied Behavioral Science*, 45: 39–58.

Langley, A. 1999. Strategies for theorizing from process data. *Academy of Management Review*, 24: 691–710.

Larsson, M. & Knudsen, M. 2021. Conditions for reflexive practices in leadership learning: The regulating role of a socio-moral order of peer interactions. *Management Learning*, online, doi: 10.1177/1350507621998859.

Leder, D. 2019. Inside insights: A phenomenology of interoception. In: Tsakiris, M. & De Preester, H. (eds.), *The Interoceptive Mind*, pp. 307–322. Oxford: Oxford University Press.

Lehmann, O.V., Hansen, M. & Hurme, H. 2020. This is the real 'death-line' AND I am still alive: A collaborative reflexivity about life trajectories. *Culture & Psychology*, 26: 819–836.

Lichterman, P. 1998. What do movements mean? The value of participant observation. *Qualitative Sociology*, 21: 401–418.

Lindebaum, D. 2017. *Emancipation Through Emotion Regulation at Work*. Cheltenham, UK and Northampton, MA, USA: Edward Elgar Publishing.

Locke, K. & Golden-Biddle, K. 1997. Constructing opportunities for contribution: Structuring intertextual coherence and 'problematizing' in organization studies. *Academy of Management Journal*, 40: 1023–1062.

Lupu, I., Spence, C. & Empson, L. 2018. When the past comes back to haunt you: The enduring influence of upbringing on the work–family decisions of professional parents. *Human Relations*, 71: 155–181.

Mahdevan, J. 2015. Caste, purity, and female dress in IT India: Embodied norm violation as reflexive ethnographic practice. *Culture and Organization*, 21: 366–385.

Marshall, J. & Reason, P. 2007. Quality in research as 'taking an attitude of inquiry'. *Management Research News*, 30: 368–380.

McDonald, J. 2016. Expanding queer reflexivity: The closet as a guiding metaphor for reflexive practice. *Management Learning*, 47: 391–406.

McLean, M., Harvey, C. & Chia, R. 2012. Reflexive practice and the making of elite business careers. *Management Learning*, 43: 385–404.

Mcleod, J. 2003. Why we interview now: Reflexivity and perspective in a longitudinal study. *International Journal of Social Research Methodology*, 6: 201–211.

Meliou, E. & Edwards, T. 2018. Relational practices and reflexivity: Exploring the responses of women entrepreneurs to changing household dynamics. *International Small Business Journal*, 36: 149–168.

Mikkelsen, E. & Clegg, S. 2019. Conceptions of conflict in organizational conflict research: Toward critical reflexivity. *Journal of Management Inquiry*, 28: 166–179.

Miller, K. 2002. The experience of emotion in the workplace: Professing in the midst of tragedy. *Management Communication Quarterly*, 15: 571–600.

Mills, T. & Kleinman, S. 1988. Emotions, reflexivity and action: An interactionist analysis. *Social Forces*, 66: 1009–1027.

Moules, N., Jardine, D., McCaffrey, G. & Brown, C. 2013. Isn't all of oncology hermeneutic? *Journal of Applied Hermeneutics*, 2013: Article 3.

Moules, N., McCaffrey, G., Field, J. & Laing, C. 2015. *Conducting Hermeneutic Research: From Philosophy to Practice*. New York: Peter Lang.

Myers, K. 2010. *Reflexive Practice: Professional Thinking for a Turbulent World*. New York: Palgrave Macmillan.

Namatende-Sakwa, L. 2018. 'Madam, are you one of them?' 'Reflexivities of discomfort' in researching an 'illicit' subject. *International Journal of Qualitative Studies in Education*, 31: 328–340.

Nicholls, R. 2009. Research and Indigenous participation: Critical reflexive methods. *International Journal of Social Research Methodology*, 12: 117–126.

Okumus, F., Altinay, L. & Roper, A. 2007. Gaining access for research: Reflections from experience. *Annals of Tourism Research*, 34: 7–26.

Parker, M. 1995. Critique in the name of what? Postmodernism and critical approaches to organization. *Organization Studies*, 16: 553–564.

Parker, S., Racz, M. & Palmer, P. 2020. Reflexive learning and performative failure. *Management Learning*, 51: 293–313.

Perry, M. & Medina, C.L. (eds.) 2015. *Methodologies of Embodiment. Inscribing Bodies in Qualitative Research*. London: Routledge.

Peticca-Harris, A., deGama, N. & Elias, S. 2016. A dynamic process model for finding informants and gaining access in qualitative research. *Organizational Research Methods*, 19: 376–401.

Pettigrew, P. 2003. Power, conflicts and resolutions: A change agent's perspective on conducting action research within a multiorganizational partnership. *Systemic Practice and Action Research*, 16: 375–391.

Polanyi, M. 1966. *The Tacit Dimension*. New York: Doubleday.

Pollner, M. 1991. Left of ethnomethodology: The rise and decline of radical reflexivity. *American Sociological Review*, 56: 370–380.

Prasad, A. 2002. The contest over meaning: Hermeneutics as an interpretive methodology for understanding texts. *Organizational Research Methods*, 5: 12–33.

Purnell, D. & Clarke, D. 2019. Finding our fathers. *Qualitative Inquiry*, 25: 907–914.

Quadt, L., Critchley, H. & Garfinkel, S. 2019. Interoception and emotion: Shared mechanisms and clinical implications. In: Tsakiris, M. & De Preester, H. (eds.), *The Interoceptive Mind*, pp. 123–143. Oxford: Oxford University Press.

Raelin, J. 2008. Emancipatory discourse and liberation. *Management Learning*, 39: 519–540.

Reynolds, M. 1998. Reflection and critical reflection in management learning. *Management Learning*, 29: 183–200.

Rhodes, C. 2009. After reflexivity: Ethics, freedom and the writing of organization studies. *Organization Studies*, 30: 653–672.

Rhodes, C. & Carlsen, A. 2018. The teaching of the other: Ethical vulnerability and generous reciprocity in the research process. *Human Relations*, 71: 1295–1318.

Ripamonti, S., Galuppo, L., Gorli, M., Scaratti, G. & Cunliffe, A.L. 2017. Pushing action research toward reflexive practice. *Journal of Management Inquiry*, 25: 55–68.

Rosen, M. 2019. Reading nearby: Literary ethnography in a postsocialist city. *Anthropology and Humanism*, 44: 70–87.

Sandberg, J. & Alvesson, M. 2011. Ways of constructing research questions: Gap-spotting or problematization? *Organization*, 18: 23–44.

Schachter, S. & Singer, J. 1962. Cognitive, social, and physiological determinants of emotional state. *Psychological Review*, 69: 379–399.

Schmutz, J., Lei, Z., Eppich, W. & Manser, T. 2018. Reflection in the heat of the moment: The role of in-action team reflexivity in health care emergency teams. *Journal of Organizational Behavior*, 39: 749–765.

Schwartz-Shea, P. & Yanow, D. 2012. *Interpretive Research Design: Concepts and Processes*. London: Routledge.

Sela-Sheffy, R. & Leshem, R. 2016. Emotion-identity talk in aggressive interactions and in reflexive accounts. *Culture & Psychology*, 22: 448–466.

Shils, E. 1981. *Tradition*. Chicago: University of Chicago Press.

Shin, Y. 2014. Positive group affect and team creativity: Mediation of team reflexivity and promotion focus. *Small Group Research*, 45: 337–364.

Simon, G. 2013. Relational ethnography: Writing and reading in research relationships. *Forum: Qualitative Social Research*, 14: Article 4.

Sklaveniti, C. & Steyaert, C. 2020. Reflecting with Pierre Bourdieu: Towards a reflexive outlook for practice-based studies of entrepreneurship. *Entrepreneurship & Regional Development*, 32: 313–333.

Steyaert, C. & Van Looy, B. (eds.) 2010. *Relational Practices, Participative Organizing*. Bingley: Emerald.

Stoddart, M. 2007. Ideology, hegemony, discourse: A critical review of theories of knowledge and power. *Social Thought and Research*, 28: 191–226.

Stringer, C. & Simmons, G. 2015. Stepping through the looking glass: Researching slavery in New Zealand's fishing industry. *Journal of Management Inquiry*, 24: 253–263.

Tayar, M. & Paisley, V. 2015. Reflexivity, critical reflection, and mindfulness in experiential learning: Developing successful international business graduates. In Taras, V. & Gonzalez-Vera, M. (eds.), *Palgrave Handbook of Experiential Learning in International Business*, pp. 464–483. Basingstoke: Palgrave Macmillan.

Thompson, F. & Perry, C. 2004. Generalising results of an action research project in one work place to other situations: Principles and practice. *European Journal of Marketing*, 38: 401–417.

Todd, J. 2020. Experiencing and embodying anxiety in spaces of academia and social research. *Gender, Place & Culture*, online, doi: 10.1080/0966369X.2020.1727862.

Troth, A., Lawrence, S., Jordan, P. & Ashkanasy, N. 2018. Interpersonal emotion regulation in the workplace: A conceptual and operational review and future research agenda. *International Journal of Management Reviews*, 20: 523–543.

Tsakiris, M. & De Preester, H. (eds.) 2019. *The Interoceptive Mind*. Oxford: Oxford University Press.

Van den Bergh, O., Zacharioudakis, N. & Petersen, S. 2019. Interoception, categorization and symptom perception. In: Tsakiris, M. & De Preester, H. (eds.), *The Interoceptive Mind*, pp. 212–226. Oxford: Oxford University Press.

van der Kolk, B. 2015. *The Body Keeps the Score*. London: Penguin Random House.

Vandevelde, P. 2010. What is the ethics of interpretation? In: Malpas, J. & Zabala, S. (eds.), *Consequences of Hermeneutics*, pp. 288–305. Evanston, IL: Northwestern University Press.

Vinten, G. 1994. Participant observation: A model for organizational investigation. *Journal of Managerial Psychology*, 9: 30–38.

Vu, M. & Burton, N. 2020. Mindful reflexivity: Unpacking the process of transformative learning in mindfulness and discernment. *Management Learning*, 51: 207–226.

Weeks, J. 2000. What do ethnographers believe? A reply to Jones. *Human Relations*, 53: 153–171.

Weick, K. 1999. Theory construction as disciplined reflexivity: Tradeoffs in the 90s. *Academy of Management Review*, 24: 797–806.

Wiley, J. 1987. The 'shock of unrecognition' as a problem in participant-observation. *Qualitative Sociology*, 10: 78–82.

Wilson, C. & Stock, J. 2019. The impact of living with long-term conditions in young adulthood on mental health and identity: What can help? *Health Expectations*, 22: 1111–1121.

Wilson, H. 2004: Towards rigour in action research: A case study in marketing planning. *European Journal of Marketing*, 38: 378–400.

Winkler, A. 2014. Resilience as reflexivity: A new understanding for work with looked-after children. *Journal of Social Work Practice*, 28: 461–478.

Winterburn, K. 2020. Dis-ease of experience – A critically reflexive account of practice. *Action Learning: Research and Practice*, 17: 232–238.

Wittman, M. & Meissner, K. 2019. The embodiment of time: How interoception shapes the perception of time. In: Tsakiris, M. & De Preester, H. (eds.), *The Interoceptive Mind*, pp. 63–79. Oxford: Oxford University Press.

Wright, A. & Hibbert, P. 2015. Threshold concepts in theory and practice. *Journal of Management Education*, 39: 443–451.

Wright, A., Middleton, S., Hibbert, P. & Brazil, V. 2020. Getting on with field research using participant deconstruction. *Organizational Research Methods*, 23: 275–295.

Wright, A. & Wright, C. 2019. When research and personal lifeworlds collide. *Research in the Sociology of Organizations*, 59: 255–273.

Index

Printed and bound by CPI Group (UK) Ltd, Croydon, CR0 4YY

09/06/2025

14685771-0001